LM

GORDON RAMSAY'S

WORLD KITCHEN

RECIPES FROM THE f WORD

Quadrille
PUBLISHING

FOOD BY

GORDON RAMSAY

WITH MARK SARGEANT

TEXT BY

EMILY QUAH

PHOTOGRAPHS BY

CHRIS TERRY

notes

All spoon measures are level unless otherwise stated:
1 tsp = 5ml spoon; 1 tbsp = 15ml spoon.

All herbs are fresh, and all pepper is freshly ground unless otherwise suggested.

I recommend using free-range eggs. If you are pregnant or in a vulnerable health group, avoid those recipes that contain raw egg whites or lightly cooked eggs.

If possible, buy unwaxed citrus fruit if you are using the zest.

Cooking times are provided as guidelines, with a description of colour or texture as appropriate. Preheat your oven and use an oven thermometer to check its accuracy.

Introduction

Food has become a lot more innovative and exciting over the past decade. Particularly in London, but also throughout the UK, we are spoilt for choice when it comes to restaurants offering enticing food from all corners of the globe. From exotic Thai curries to classic French fare, you are likely to find a variety of restaurants offering different styles of cooking in most towns and cities.

My work commitments over the past few years have taken me to lots of far-flung places, but every time I come home, I am continually impressed by the quality of food served at my favourite local restaurants. Like many of you, I love a good Friday night curry. Granted, my local 'curry house' boasts a Michelin star of its own, but I find that the food can be just as good as some of the dishes I sampled during my recent trip to

However, it's not all about Michelin stars. It is true that there are still restaurants serving inferior food, but fortunately for everyone, the current credit crisis has forced restaurants to re-evaluate their business and deliver value to their customers. This not only means offering consistent good food at reasonable prices, but also a good ambience, friendly and attentive service, and general cleanliness. It's all common sense stuff that has somehow evaded the conscience of many a restaurant manager until now.

Another positive 'side effect' of the financial crisis is that entertaining at home is on the up. I'm hoping that as a consequence, we – as a nation – are cooking more. And as our palates adapt and evolve, so too should our cooking repertoire. The variety of exotic ingredients now available at most supermarkets has made it easy and convenient for us to cook a wide range of dishes, from an Italian osso buco to Middle Eastern dolmades. Any ingredient that is not found at a major grocery chain may require a trip to an Oriental, Middle Eastern or Asian food store, but think of these sorties less as an inconvenience and more a route to discovery. After all, the best way to learn about unusual ingredients is by cooking them.

For this book, I've chosen a selection of my favourite dishes from ten very different cuisines – from the best cuisines in Europe to those from China, Thailand and other far-away lands. Each cuisine is tied to a culture steeped in tradition and local custom, so my limited selection of recipes can only be a taster to whet the appetite. The recipes are also my take on these dishes, often with a little innovative twist to make them more accessible and easy to cook at home. I hope that they will inspire you to step out of your comfort zone and try something new every week. Enjoy...

FRENCH

ALTHOUGH MY FOOD HAS CHANGED AND NOW HAS A
MORE ECLECTIC STYLE, MY HEART STILL BELONGS TO
FRANCE. MY FORMATIVE YEARS WERE SPENT TRAINING
WITH THE ROUX BROTHERS AND A THREE-YEAR STINT
IN PARIS TAUGHT ME A GREAT DEAL ABOUT FRENCH
CUISINE. WHENEVER I RETURN, I GO TO THE MARKETS
– THE AMAZING PRODUCE NEVER CEASES TO INSPIRE
ME AND I'M BUZZING WITH IDEAS WHEN I GET BACK
HOME. THERE ARE SO MANY FANTASTIC DISHES AND,
OF COURSE, THERE'S THE WINE! OVER THE YEARS,
WE HAVE LEARNED A LOT FROM FRENCH COOKING AND
WE SHOULD NEVER FORGET THAT. YES, THINGS HAVE
MOVED ON DRAMATICALLY, BUT WITHOUT AUGUSTE
ESCOFFIER OR FERNAND POINT WHERE WOULD WE BE?

Brandade on garlic toasts

THIS IS MY TAKE ON THE CLASSIC brandade. Instead of salted cod, which calls for lengthy soaking, I gently poach fresh cod in olive oil to achieve a tender and succulent result. For a delicious starter, serve the brandade and garlic toasts with a lightly dressed mixed salad and chilled crisp, dry white wine.

SERVES 6–8

Brandade:
300g cod fillet, skinned
150ml olive oil
1/2 tsp rock salt
2 thyme sprigs
350g potatoes, such as
    Maris Piper
150ml double cream
150ml whole milk
2 garlic cloves, peeled and sliced
sea salt and black pepper
2 basil sprigs, leaves shredded

Garlic toasts:
4–6 small baguettes
    (or 1–2 large ones)
1 large garlic clove, peeled and
    halved
extra virgin olive oil, to drizzle

Check the fish for small bones, removing any with kitchen tweezers. Place the cod, olive oil, rock salt and a thyme sprig in a small saucepan. Place the pan over the lowest possible heat and cook very gently for 8–10 minutes until the fish begins to flake easily. Leave to cool, then drain well, saving the oil. Flake into large pieces.

Peel the potatoes and cut into 2cm cubes. Place in a saucepan with the cream, milk, garlic, remaining thyme sprig and some seasoning. Simmer for 10–12 minutes until soft. Drain, discarding the thyme, then mash lightly. Mix with the flaked cod, adding some of the reserved oil, and season with salt and pepper to taste. Allow to cool, then stir in the shredded basil. The brandade is best served at room temperature.

When just about ready to serve, preheat the grill to high. Thinly slice the baguettes on the diagonal (or halve small ones, if you prefer) and lay them on a baking sheet. Grill for about 1 minute (rounded sides up if halved) until lightly golden, then turn them over and rub the non-toasted sides with the garlic. Drizzle with extra virgin olive oil and grill until golden and crisp. Don't leave unattended as the toasts can burn easily.

Spoon the brandade into small serving bowls and grind over some pepper. Place the garlic toasts alongside for everyone to help themselves at the table. Or serve the toasts topped with the brandade, if you prefer.

Moules marinière

ROPE-GROWN MUSSELS are now widely available pretty much all year round, which means that we can enjoy this lovely dish any time. It is equally suited to warm and chilly days. Serve in deep soup bowls with home-made chips if you like, plus mayonnaise and lots of crusty bread to mop up the flavourful juices.

SERVES 4

1kg live mussels
1 onion, peeled and finely chopped
1 shallot, peeled and finely chopped
1 garlic clove, peeled and finely chopped
1 bay leaf
3 thyme sprigs
handful of flat-leaf parsley, stalks separated,
    leaves chopped
200ml dry white wine
black pepper

Scrub the mussels clean under cold running water, scraping off any barnacles with a knife and tugging away any beards. Check over the mussels, discarding any that are cracked or open and do not close when sharply tapped. Rinse well and set aside.

Place the onion, shallot, garlic, bay leaf, thyme, parsley stalks and wine in a large pan. Bring to the boil, then tip in the mussels and cover the pan with a tight-fitting lid. Give the pan one or two shakes, then let the mussels steam for 3–4 minutes until they have opened. Discard any that remain closed. Season with a good grinding of pepper. Mussels are naturally salty so you probably won't need to add salt.

Divide the mussels and cooking juices between warm large bowls and sprinkle with the chopped parsley. Serve immediately, remembering to provide bowls for the discarded empty shells.

Pan-frying scallops

Sweet, juicy, fresh scallops need to be treated with respect to retain their lovely succulence – overcook them and they turn horribly tough and rubbery. I use this simple technique to ensure quick, even cooking.

Cut the scallops in half horizontally into discs. Heat a thin film of olive oil in a heavy-based frying pan until really hot. Season the scallops with sea salt and black pepper and lay them in the pan, clockwise fashion in a circle. Fry for 1 minute until golden at the edges, then turn them in the same order that you placed them in the pan. Cook for no longer than a minute on the other side – the scallops should feel quite bouncy when lightly pressed. Squeeze over a little lemon juice and serve at once.

Pan-fried scallops with leeks vinaigrette

TENDER LEEKS AND VERY FRESH SCALLOPS both have a delightful natural sweetness and are perfect partners. A tangy mustardy vinaigrette provides a welcome contrast for this dish.

SERVES 4

12 large scallops, cleaned
2 tbsp olive oil
sea salt and black pepper
squeeze of lemon juice

Leeks vinaigrette:
8 medium leeks, white part only, trimmed
125ml extra virgin olive oil
1 tbsp Dijon mustard
1 tbsp cider or white wine vinegar
pinch of caster sugar (optional)

To finish:
flat-leaf parsley leaves

Set the cleaned scallops aside at room temperature while you prepare the leeks vinaigrette.

Thinly slice the white leeks, then wash thoroughly, drain and pat dry. Heat 2 tbsp extra virgin olive oil in a wide sauté pan over a medium heat and add the leeks with some seasoning. Sweat them, stirring occasionally, for 6–8 minutes until they are soft but not coloured.

Meanwhile, make the vinaigrette. Put the remaining extra virgin olive oil, mustard, vinegar and a pinch each of salt and pepper into a screw-topped jar. Seal and shake well, then taste and adjust the seasoning, adding a pinch of sugar if necessary.

When the leeks are soft, add a few tablespoonfuls of the vinaigrette to the pan and toss until the leeks are nicely coated.

Now heat the olive oil in a wide frying pan and pan-fry the scallops following my guide (on the preceding pages).

Spoon the leeks vinaigrette onto warm plates. Arrange the scallops on top and drizzle a little more vinaigrette around the plate (keep any remaining dressing in the fridge and use to drizzle over salads). Garnish the scallops with parsley leaves and serve immediately.

Tuna provençale

I ADORE THE FLAVOURS OF PROVENCE, particularly the abundant use of fresh vegetables and herbs in many classic dishes. This healthy tuna and Mediterranean vegetable bake is light and flavourful, but you do need to get very fresh tuna especially if – like me – you prefer the fish on the rare side.

SERVES 4

4 fresh line-caught tuna steaks, about 180g each and 2cm thick
2–3 tbsp olive oil, plus extra to drizzle
1 red onion, peeled and chopped
4 garlic cloves, peeled and finely chopped
1 yellow pepper, cored, deseeded and chopped
1 red pepper, cored, deseeded and chopped
sea salt and black pepper
2 medium courgettes, trimmed and roughly chopped
400g tin chopped plum tomatoes
1 thyme sprig
1 rosemary sprig
50g pitted black olives
1 lemon, thinly sliced
handful of basil leaves, shredded (optional)

Preheat the oven to 200°C/Fan 180°C/Gas 6. Trim the tuna steaks if necessary and set aside.

Heat the olive oil in a wide pan. Add the onion, garlic and peppers with some seasoning and sauté over a medium-high heat for 5–6 minutes until they begin to soften but not colour. Add the courgettes, stir well and cook for another 2–3 minutes. Now add the chopped tomatoes, thyme, rosemary and olives, mix well and bring to a simmer. Cook for a few minutes, then transfer to a wide ovenproof dish.

Rub the tuna steaks all over with salt, pepper and a little drizzle of olive oil. Overlap the tuna steaks on top of the vegetables and tuck the lemon slices in between. Add a generous grinding of pepper then place in the oven. Bake for about 8–10 minutes until the tuna is cooked to medium rare – the steaks should feel slightly springy when pressed. If you prefer tuna well done, bake for a further 5–10 minutes until they feel just firm.

Scatter shredded basil over the dish, if you like, and serve straight away. Delicious simply with good country bread, or with sautéed potatoes.

Confit duck leg
with sautéed potatoes

THIS TRADITIONAL DISH IS FROM PÉRIGORD, a region famed for its duck and goose foie gras. There, succulent and tender duck confit is customarily served with a salad and potatoes – either sautéed in the same flavourful fat in which the duck was cooked, or in a hearty gratin. A scrumptious, rich dish for the occasional indulgent meal.

SERVES 4

Confit duck legs:
4 duck legs
rock salt
handful of thyme sprigs
3 garlic cloves, peeled and sliced
2 bay leaves
2 x 350g tins duck or goose fat

Sautéed potatoes:
500g small waxy potatoes, such
    as Charlotte, peeled and halved
1 rosemary sprig, leaves finely
    chopped
sea salt and black pepper

Sprinkle the duck legs all over with rock salt and leave to stand at room temperature for an hour.

Preheat the oven to 140°C/Fan 120°C/Gas 1. Rinse off the salt from the duck and pat dry with kitchen paper. Place the duck legs in a roasting pan in which they fit quite snugly and add the thyme, garlic and bay leaves. Melt the duck fat in a saucepan over a low heat. When it is translucent, carefully pour it over the duck legs, to cover them completely.

Cover the pan with foil and carefully place in the oven. Cook slowly for about 2 hours until the meat is very tender, making sure the legs remain covered by the fat. The duck is ready when the meat slips easily away from the bone. Remove from the oven.

Turn the oven setting up to 200°C/Fan 180°C/Gas 6. Lift the cooked duck legs out of the fat and place skin-side down in a roasting pan; reserve the fat. Roast the duck legs in the hot oven for 15–20 minutes, turning halfway. The skin will crisp up beautifully, while the meat remains tender.

Meanwhile, parboil the potatoes in a saucepan of boiling salted water for 4–5 minutes until half-cooked. Tip into a colander to drain and leave for a few minutes to dry off; this will help them to crispen. Place a non-stick frying pan over a medium-high heat and add a thin layer of the saved duck fat. When hot, add the potatoes with the rosemary and season well. Cook until the underside is golden brown, then turn and sauté for a few minutes until the potatoes are nicely coloured and crisp all over, yet fluffy inside.

Serve the confit duck legs with the sautéed potatoes. Accompany with some grainy mustard and French beans, if you like.

Guinea fowl braised in cider with caramelised apples

THE NORMANDY REGION BOASTS SUPERB PRODUCTS, including wonderful cream, butter, apples and Calvados – all of which are ingredients for the classic *poulet à la Normande*. For a change, I've replaced the chicken with guinea fowl, which I find to be more flavourful and well suited to the rich and creamy sauce.

SERVES 4

2 guinea fowl, about 800g each, jointed
sea salt and black pepper
2–3 tbsp olive oil
2 thin rashers streaky bacon, chopped
300ml medium cider
100ml Calvados or brandy
250ml double cream
few thyme sprigs, leaves stripped
500g firm, tart apples (about 3)
30g butter
1–2 tsp caster sugar
squeeze of lemon juice, to taste
30g walnuts, toasted and lightly crushed
handful of flat-leaf parsley, leaves chopped

Preheat the oven to 200°C/Fan 180°C/Gas 6. Season the guinea fowl joints with salt and pepper. Heat a thin layer of olive oil in a wide flameproof casserole until hot. Brown the guinea fowl in batches for 2–3 minutes on each side until evenly coloured, removing the pieces to a plate when they are ready.

Add the bacon to the casserole and fry until lightly golden brown. Pour in the cider and Calvados, bring to the boil and let bubble until reduced by one-third. Stir in the cream and thyme leaves.

Return the guinea fowl pieces to the casserole, put the lid on and place in the oven. Braise for 30–45 minutes until the guinea fowl is tender and just cooked through; remove the breast pieces after 20–25 minutes to avoid overcooking and return them for the last 5 minutes to warm through.

About 15 minutes before you will be ready to serve the guinea fowl, peel, core and thickly slice the apples into rings. Melt the butter in a large frying pan. Sprinkle the apple slices with sugar and fry them in the butter for about 4–5 minutes on each side until golden brown.

When the guinea fowl is ready, remove the pieces to a warm plate. If you find the sauce too thin, boil it until reduced and thickened to the desired consistency. Season to taste with salt, pepper and a little lemon juice.

Return the guinea fowl to the sauce and garnish with the caramelised apples. Sprinkle the walnuts and chopped parsley on top before serving.

Navarin of lamb with spring vegetables

THIS ELEGANT DISH IS AN EASTER SPECIALITY in France. Tender braised lamb neck fillet and a medley of spring vegetables are brought together in a flavourful, light sauce. The dish does take a little time to make, but it certainly isn't difficult. It is important to brown the meat well and to use good-quality lamb stock.

SERVES 4

16 baby turnips, trimmed
16 baby carrots, peeled or scrubbed
16 baby leeks, trimmed
100g peas, thawed if frozen
120g broad beans, skinned
12 baby onions or small shallots, peeled
sea salt and black pepper
800g lamb neck fillet
20g plain flour, to dust
2 tbsp olive oil
300ml light red wine, such as Beaujolais
2 garlic cloves, peeled and chopped
1 bay leaf
3 thyme sprigs
3 rosemary sprigs
400ml chicken stock
50g cold butter, cut into small pieces
1 tbsp caster sugar
2 tbsp balsamic vinegar
small handful of tarragon, leaves picked

For the vegetables, have a bowl of iced water ready and bring a large pan of salted water to the boil. Working in batches, blanch the turnips for 3 minutes, then remove to the iced water with a slotted spoon to refresh. Once cooled, scoop them out onto a plate. Repeat the process with the rest of the vegetables, blanching the carrots for 4 minutes, the leeks for 5 minutes, the peas and broad beans for 1 minute and, finally, the baby onions for 8–10 minutes.

Cut the lamb into 3–3.5cm chunks, dust with flour and season generously with salt and pepper. Heat the olive oil in a flameproof casserole or wide, heavy-based pan and fry the lamb, in batches if necessary, until browned all over. Tip the meat into a colander set over a bowl to catch the juices.

Place the casserole back on the heat and add the wine, garlic, bay leaf, thyme and rosemary. Boil vigorously until reduced to a sticky syrup, then pour in the stock. Return the lamb to the casserole, along with any meat juices from the bowl. Bring to a simmer and skim off excess fat. Turn the heat right down and simmer very gently for about 2 hours, skimming every so often.

When the lamb is tender, remove the meat to a plate with a slotted spoon. Increase the heat and reduce the sauce down to a light coating consistency. Now whisk in the butter, a piece at a time. Season well with salt and pepper to taste, adding a little sugar and balsamic vinegar for a little sweetness and acidity if you like.

Return the lamb to the sauce and stir in the blanched vegetables. Bring to a simmer and reheat gently for 4–5 minutes. Divide between warm shallow bowls and scatter over the tarragon leaves. Serve at once.

Lemon **soufflé**

IT IS REALLY NOT THAT TRICKY TO MAKE A SOUFFLÉ and I'm determined to prove it! Those of you who shy away from them, please give this recipe a go. The secret lies in making a thick soufflé base and adequately whisking the egg whites until they are firm and glossy. Also, it is important to resist opening the oven door until the soufflé is ready, otherwise it is liable to collapse.

SERVES 4

40g unsalted butter, well
    softened, for brushing
100g caster sugar, plus extra
    to dust
150ml whole milk
100ml double cream
3 large egg yolks
15g plain flour
10g cornflour
4 large egg whites
finely grated zest and juice of
    2 lemons
icing sugar, to dust

Brush 4 individual soufflé dishes (250ml capacity) with the softened butter, using upward vertical strokes, including the rims. Chill for a few minutes, then brush with a second layer of butter. Sprinkle some caster sugar into each dish, shaking and tipping the dish to dust the butter-coated base and sides evenly. Tip out any excess and chill until needed.

For the soufflé base, pour the milk and cream into a heavy-based pan and slowly bring to just below the boil, then remove from the heat. Meanwhile, whisk the egg yolks and 50g caster sugar together in a large bowl until pale and thick. Sift the flour and cornflour together onto the yolk mixture and whisk again until smooth. Now, slowly add the creamy milk, whisking as you go. Pour the mixture back into the pan and stir constantly over a low heat with a wooden spoon for 5 minutes or so, until it is smooth and quite thick. Set aside to cool. Preheat the oven to 200°C/Fan 180°C/Gas 6.

In a large clean bowl, whisk the egg whites to stiff peaks. Add a few drops of lemon juice, then whisk again. Gradually whisk in the remaining 50g sugar, a spoonful at a time, until you have a very thick, glossy mixture.

Stir the lemon zest and juice into the soufflé base, then whisk in a third of the egg white mix to loosen the mixture. Now carefully fold in the rest of the egg white, using a large metal spoon, until evenly incorporated.

Spoon the mixture into the prepared dishes, filling them to the top, then tap each once on the work surface to get rid of any air bubbles. Gently smooth the surface with a small palette knife. Run the tip of the palette knife around the inside edge of the dish, then place on a baking sheet. Bake in the middle of the oven for 15–18 minutes or until risen with a slight wobble in the middle. Dust with icing sugar and serve straight away.

Chocolate crêpes with Chantilly cream

THIN CRÊPES ARE A SPECIALITY OF BRITTANY. Originally crêpes were always savoury, made with locally milled buckwheat flour, but sweet ones have gained popularity over the years. My cream-filled chocolate version, drizzled with chocolate sauce, is satisfyingly rich. If you don't have a crêpe pan, just use a wide non-stick frying pan.

SERVES 6–8

Crêpes:
100g plain flour
25g cocoa powder
$1/4$ tsp fine sea salt
1 tbsp caster sugar
2 medium eggs, lightly beaten
1 tbsp melted butter, plus a few knobs for cooking
300ml whole milk
1 tsp vanilla extract

Chocolate sauce:
100g good-quality dark chocolate (about 70% cocoa solids)
15g unsalted butter
$1^1/2$ tbsp clear honey
70ml whole milk

Crème chantilly:
250ml double cream
2–3 tbsp icing sugar
1 tsp vanilla extract

To serve:
4 tbsp flaked or nibbed almonds, lightly toasted
candied orange zest (see page 102), optional

For the crêpes, sift the flour, cocoa powder and salt into a bowl and stir in the sugar. Make a well in the centre and tip in the beaten eggs, melted butter, milk and vanilla extract. Whisk to combine the ingredients and form a smooth batter, but try not to overwork the mixture. Leave to stand or chill for at least 30 minutes.

For the chocolate sauce, break the chocolate into small pieces and place in a heatproof bowl over a pan of simmering water. Add the butter and honey and allow to melt, stirring from time to time. Remove from the heat and gradually whisk in the milk until you have a smooth sauce. If necessary, warm the sauce slightly before serving.

For the crème chantilly, in a bowl, whip the cream with the icing sugar and vanilla extract to soft peaks. Cover and chill until ready to serve.

To cook the crêpes, place a non-stick crêpe pan over a medium heat and add a knob of butter. When melted, tilt the pan so that the butter coats the base. Add a small ladleful of batter and swirl to evenly coat the base of the pan in a thin layer. Cook for about $1^1/2$ minutes until the batter is set and golden brown underneath. Flip over to cook the other side for a minute. Transfer to a warm plate and wrap in a tea towel to keep warm. Repeat with the rest of the batter, stacking the crêpes interleaved with greaseproof paper in the tea towel as they are cooked.

To serve, spread a layer of crème chantilly over one half of each crêpe, scatter with a few toasted almonds. Fold the plain half of the crêpe over the filling to enclose, then fold again into quarters. Place one filled crêpe on each serving plate and drizzle over the chocolate sauce. Scatter over a few toasted almonds, and if you wish, top with some candied orange zest.

Raspberry tart

EXQUISITE PASTRIES AND TARTS IN PATISSERIES and bakeries across France never fail to seduce passers-by. I'm always reminded of them by this irresistible, glistening *tarte aux framboise*. You will have more pastry and possibly more vanilla cream than you need (it isn't practical to make a smaller amount), but you can always make some little tartlets.

SERVES 8–10

Sweet flan pastry:
125g unsalted butter,
    softened to room temperature
90g caster sugar
1 large egg
250g plain flour, plus extra to dust
1 tbsp ice-cold water (if needed)

Vanilla cream:
250ml whole milk
1/2 vanilla pod, slit lengthways
    and seeds scraped out
50g caster sugar
20g cornflour
3 large egg yolks
100ml double cream

Topping:
about 700g raspberries, wiped
    or brushed clean (rather than
    washed)
2–3 tbsp seedless raspberry jam,
    to glaze
1 tbsp hot water (if needed)

To make the pastry, whiz the butter and sugar in a food processor until just combined. Add the egg and whiz for 30 seconds. Tip in the flour and process for a few seconds until the dough just comes together, adding a little water if needed. Knead lightly on a floured surface. Shape into a disc, wrap in cling film and chill for 30 minutes.

Roll out the pastry on a lightly floured surface to the thickness of a £1 coin. Use it to line a 23–25cm tart tin with removable base, trimming off the excess pastry around the edges. Chill for at least 30 minutes.

For the vanilla cream, put the milk, vanilla seeds and pod in a heavy-based pan with 1 tbsp of the sugar. Heat slowly until almost boiling. Meanwhile, beat the remaining sugar, cornflour and egg yolks together in a bowl. As the milk begins to scald, slowly trickle it onto the egg mix, stirring all the time. Rinse out the pan. Pass the mixture through a fine sieve into the pan. Stir over a low heat until it forms a thick custard. Pass through a sieve into a clean bowl and let cool, stirring occasionally, to prevent a skin forming.

Preheat the oven to 200°C/Fan 180°C /Gas 6 with a baking sheet inside. Line the pastry case with greaseproof paper and baking beans. Place the tart tin on the baking sheet and bake for 15–20 minutes. Remove the paper and beans and return to the oven for 5 minutes to finish cooking the base. Leave to cool for 10 minutes, then unmould and cool on a wire rack.

Whip the cream to soft peaks. Beat the cooled vanilla custard slightly to loosen it, then fold in the cream. Chill until ready to serve. Spread a thin layer of vanilla cream in the pastry case. Arrange the raspberries on top. Warm the raspberry jam a little, thinning it with the hot water if necessary, then brush over the berries to glaze. Best eaten slightly chilled on the day.

ITALIAN

I AM LUCKY ENOUGH TO HAVE WORKED A LOT IN ITALY,
PARTICULARLY IN TUSCANY AND SARDINIA. ITALIANS
ARE VERY PROUD AND PASSIONATE ABOUT THEIR
INGREDIENTS AND FOOD. ALMOST EVERY TOWN AND
VILLAGE HAS ITS OWN PASTA AND EACH ONE IS MADE
SPECIFICALLY FOR THE SAUCE IT IS SUPPOSED TO GO
WITH. THEY ALSO HAVE DEFINITE VIEWS ABOUT HOW
THEIR FOOD SHOULD BE EATEN. SHOULD YOU MAKE THE
MISTAKE OF ASKING FOR PARMESAN WITH A PASTA DISH
CONTAINING FISH, YOU'LL BE TOLD IN NO UNCERTAIN
TERMS THAT IT IS NOT THE DONE THING. TO ITALIANS,
FOOD IS SOMETHING THAT YOU GROW UP WITH AND AN
IMPORTANT PART OF LIFE, NOT JUST SOMETHING TO
KEEP YOU ALIVE. GOOD COOKING IS IN THEIR BLOOD.

Griddled courgettes
with prosciutto

PERFECT AS A SUMMER STARTER, or as part of an antipasto spread, this lovely dish is incredibly easy to make. You do, however, need to use very fresh courgettes and a good-quality cured ham – ideally prosciutto di San Daniele.

SERVES 4

4 large courgettes, trimmed
2 tbsp olive oil
sea salt and black pepper
200g good-quality prosciutto, thinly sliced
2 tbsp pine nuts, toasted
handful of flat-leaf parsley, leaves picked

Sweet and sour dressing:
2 tbsp red wine vinegar
1–2 tbsp blossom honey
juice of 1/2 lemon
6 tbsp extra virgin olive oil
few thyme sprigs, leaves picked

First, make the sweet and sour dressing. In a small bowl, whisk together the wine vinegar, 1 tbsp honey and most of the lemon juice to combine, then gradually whisk in the extra virgin olive oil. Stir in the thyme leaves and season with salt and pepper. Taste for seasoning, adding more honey or lemon if you feel it is needed. The dressing should have the perfect balance of sweet, salty and sour.

Cut the courgettes on the diagonal into 1.5cm thick slices. Tip them into a large bowl, add the olive oil, salt and pepper and toss well to coat. Heat up a griddle pan over a medium-high heat, then cook the courgette slices for 3–4 minutes on each side until they are lightly browned and tender.

Arrange the slices of prosciutto and courgette on individual plates. Drizzle over the sweet and sour dressing and scatter over the pine nuts and parsley leaves. Serve warm or at room temperature.

Wild mushrooms on griddled polenta with pecorino

THIS IS THE ITALIAN ANSWER to our mushrooms on toast. Griddled polenta is a brilliant base for sautéed flavourful mushrooms and when served as a generous portion, it is substantial enough for a lunch with a leafy salad on the side. Do use a good mix of wild mushrooms when in season. At other times of the year, buy a selection of portabello, oyster and brown chestnut mushrooms.

SERVES 4

200g instant polenta
1.2 litres water
sea salt and black pepper
2 tbsp olive oil, plus extra for brushing
500g mixed wild mushrooms, cleaned
4 garlic cloves, peeled and chopped
25g butter
few oregano sprigs, leaves picked
2–3 tbsp plain flour, to dust
pecorino shavings, to garnish

First, prepare the polenta. Pour the water into a medium saucepan, salt lightly and bring to the boil. Add the polenta gradually in a thin, steady stream, whisking constantly. Keep stirring for about 5 minutes until the polenta thickens and all the water has been absorbed. When ready, remove from the heat, season well with salt and pepper and tip onto a lightly oiled baking tray. Using a palette knife, spread the polenta evenly, to a 2cm thickness. Leave to cool and set for 30 minutes.

When you are just about ready to serve, halve any larger mushrooms. Place a large frying pan over a high heat. When hot, add the olive oil followed by the mushrooms and fry quickly until they begin to colour. Stir in the garlic and butter with some seasoning and half the oregano leaves. Continue to fry the mushrooms over a high heat until any liquid released has been cooked off. Take the pan off the heat; keep warm.

Put a griddle pan over a medium heat. Cut the polenta into 8–10cm squares and dust with a little flour, then brush the griddle with olive oil. Griddle the polenta slices for 2–3 minutes on each side, until they begin to colour slightly. If cooking in batches, keep warm in a low oven.

To serve, place the griddled polenta slices on warm plates and top with the sautéed mushrooms. Scatter over shavings of pecorino and the remaining oregano leaves and serve immediately.

Shaping
ravioli

Lay one sheet of pasta on a clean surface, with a long edge towards you. Place teaspoonfuls of the filling along one half of the sheet (closest to you), leaving about 2cm between the filling mounds and a 3cm margin at the edge. Lightly brush the area around the filling and the rest of the pasta sheet with egg wash. Fold the edge of the pasta over the filling to enclose the mounds and press the pasta down around them to seal and exclude any air gaps. Fold the pasta over again and press down between the mounds of filling. Using a fluted pasta cutter or sharp knife, cut between the filling moulds to make the ravioli. Repeat with the rest and keep covered with a clean tea towel until ready to cook.

Spinach, ricotta and pine nut ravioli with sage butter

MAKING RAVIOLI IS TRULY SATISFYING and fun – especially if you get others involved. In Italy, this typically happens, with the matriarch in charge of quality control. You should have enough filling here for about 20 ravioli. Any pasta dough that isn't used can be re-rolled into thin sheets and cut into thick strips to make pappardelle or tagliatelle.

SERVES 4–5

Pasta dough:
pinch of saffron strands
1 tbsp boiling water
550g Italian '00' flour
1/4 tsp fine sea salt
4 medium eggs, plus 6 egg yolks
2 tbsp olive oil

Filling:
2 tbsp olive oil
2 garlic cloves, peeled and finely chopped
500g spinach leaves
15g butter
1/4 tsp freshly grated nutmeg
sea salt and black pepper
150g ricotta cheese
75g Parmesan, freshly grated
75g pine nuts, lightly toasted
squeeze of lemon juice, to taste
beaten egg, for brushing

Sage butter:
75g unsalted butter, diced
2 tbsp double cream
6 sage sprigs, leaves shredded

To serve:
Parmesan, for grating

For the pasta, lightly crush the saffron in a bowl, pour on the boiling water and leave to infuse until cooled. Put the rest of the ingredients into a food processor, add the saffron water and whiz until the mix resembles coarse crumbs; add a little more water if needed. Tip into a bowl and press into a ball with your hands. Turn onto a lightly floured surface and knead until smooth. The dough should be soft but not sticky; if it feels too wet, knead in a little more flour. Wrap in cling film and chill for 30 minutes.

To make the filling, heat the olive oil in a large frying pan and fry the garlic until lightly golden. Add the spinach and cook for 2–3 minutes until the liquid released has been absorbed. Increase the heat slightly and stir in the butter, nutmeg and seasoning. Drain and roughly chop the spinach. In a large bowl, beat together the ricotta, Parmesan and toasted pine nuts. Stir in the spinach and a touch of lemon juice. Taste and adjust the seasoning if necessary, then cover and chill for at least 30 minutes.

Cut the pasta into 8 pieces, roll into balls and keep each wrapped until needed. Using a pasta machine, roll each ball into a long sheet, about 80 x 13cm, passing it repeatedly through the rollers and narrowing the setting gradually until you reach the thinnest setting. Cover with a damp tea towel. To shape the ravioli, follow my guide (on the preceding pages).

For the sage butter, melt the butter in a saucepan and heat until it begins to brown. Take off the heat and let stand for 1 minute, then strain through a fine sieve into a clean pan. Heat slowly, then stir in the cream and sage.

Bring a large pan of lightly salted water to the boil, add the ravioli and cook for 2–3 minutes. Drain well and toss with the sage butter. Grate over a little extra Parmesan and serve at once.

5 ways with pizza

Pizza bases

Using an electric mixer fitted with a dough hook,
mix 500g strong plain flour with a 7g sachet fast-
action dried yeast, 1 tsp fine sea salt and 100ml warm
water. Slowly add more water (up to 150ml) just until
the dough starts to come together. Knead in the mixer
for 1 minute, then briefly on a lightly floured surface
until smooth and elastic. Transfer to a lightly oiled
bowl, cover with cling film and leave to rise in a warm
place until doubled in size. Knead briefly on a floured
surface, then divide in half and roll each piece out to
a 20cm circle. Place on a lightly oiled baking tray.

MAKES 2

Tomato sauce

Gently sauté 2 finely chopped garlic cloves and 1 finely
chopped onion in 2 tbsp olive oil in a medium pan until
softened. Add a 400g tin chopped tomatoes, 100g diced
cherry tomatoes and 1 tbsp tomato purée. Simmer
gently for 40 minutes or until reduced and quite thick.

Pizza **Margherita**

Heat the oven to 220°C/Fan 200°C/Gas 7. Spread the tomato sauce (see left) over the pizza bases, top with 250g thinly sliced mozzarella and scatter over some basil leaves. Season well and drizzle lightly with olive oil. Bake for 15–20 minutes until the crust is golden. MAKES 2

Parma ham and marinated **artichoke pizza**

Heat the oven to 220°C/Fan 200°C/Gas 7. Melt 20g butter in a pan and add 400g quartered plum tomatoes, 1 finely diced red chilli, a handful of chopped oregano leaves, 1 tsp sugar and some seasoning. Cook for 5–7 minutes, then stir in 1 tsp red wine vinegar. Cool slightly. Spoon the cooked tomato mixture over the pizza bases and top each with 6–8 finely sliced marinated artichokes, a few slices of Parma ham and a handful of black olives. Drizzle over a little olive oil and season lightly. Bake for 15–20 minutes until the crust is golden. Serve topped with a handful of shaved Parmesan and a scattering of rocket leaves. MAKES 2

Pizza bianca with **four cheeses**

Heat the oven to 180°C/Fan 160°C/Gas 4. Put 8 large unpeeled garlic cloves in an ovenproof dish. Drizzle with olive oil, season and roast for 20–25 minutes until soft. Squeeze the soft flesh from the skins into a bowl and mash with 1 tbsp finely chopped rosemary, 3–4 tbsp truffle oil (or good-quality olive oil) and some seasoning. Increase the oven temperature to 220°C/Fan 200°C/Gas 7. Spread the garlic paste thinly over the pizza bases and top each with a generous handful each of freshly grated Parmesan, goat's cheese and Gorgonzola, and a few mozzarella slices. Bake for 15–20 minutes until the crust is golden. MAKES 2

Roasted **tomato** and **mushroom pizza**

Heat the oven to 180°C/Fan 160°C/Gas 4. Place 350–400g cherry tomatoes on a baking tray, drizzle with 2 tbsp olive oil and season with salt and pepper. Roast for 8–10 minutes until the tomatoes are soft but still holding their shape; remove and set aside. Increase the oven temperature to 220°C/Fan 200°C/Gas 7. Melt 20g butter in a frying pan and sauté 200g sliced mixed mushrooms with 1 tsp chopped thyme leaves over a medium-high heat for 4–6 minutes until softened and any moisture released has cooked off. Cool slightly. Spread the tomato sauce (see left) over the pizza bases. Top with the sautéed mushrooms, 120g goat's cheese, 125g thinly sliced mozzarella and the roasted cherry tomatoes. Drizzle with olive oil and season well. Bake for 15–20 minutes until the crust is golden. MAKES 2

Mini **salami** and **roasted pepper pizzas**

Heat the oven to 220°C/Fan 200°C/Gas 7. Blitz 1/2 x 350g jar roasted peppers with 2 chopped garlic cloves, 50g freshly grated Parmesan, 35g toasted pine nuts, a handful of basil leaves, 100ml extra virgin olive oil and some seasoning to a paste in a food processor. Using a 6cm pastry cutter, cut the pizza dough into rounds. Spread each with a little red pepper paste, then top with the remaining roasted peppers (from the jar) and a slice of spicy salami. Sprinkle with Parmesan and bake for 12–15 minutes until the crust is golden. MAKES 14

seafood risotto

GOOD RISOTTO RICE AND A FLAVOURFUL STOCK are essential for a superb risotto. For this one, I've enhanced the flavour of the fish stock with the juices from a pan of steamed mussels. The mussels are shelled and added to the rice at the end. I've kept the seafood to a simple trio of mussels, prawns and squid, but feel free to serve the risotto topped with a pan-fried fillet of John Dory, red mullet or bream.

SERVES 6–8

300g live mussels, scrubbed clean and de-bearded
200ml water
300ml dry white wine
800ml fish or chicken stock
pinch of saffron strands
2 tbsp olive oil
40g butter
1 small head of fennel, trimmed and finely chopped
1 shallot, peeled and finely chopped
1 garlic clove, peeled and finely chopped
350g risotto rice, such as Arborio, Carnaroli or Vialone Nano
300g peeled raw prawns
200g baby squid, cleaned and sliced
finely grated zest of 1 lemon
sea salt and black pepper
handful of flat-leaf parsley, leaves chopped

Check over the mussels, discarding any that are cracked or open and do not close when sharply tapped. Pour the water and 200ml of the wine into a large saucepan and bring to the boil over a high heat. Tip in the mussels, cover the pan with a tight-fitting lid and give it a few shakes. Cook for 2–3 minutes until the mussels have opened. Drain them in a colander set on top of a saucepan to collect the juices. Shell the mussels and set aside, discarding any that remain closed. Add the stock and saffron strands to the mussel juices and bring to a simmer; keep it at a low simmer.

Meanwhile, heat the olive oil and half the butter in a large saucepan. Add the fennel, shallot and garlic and fry until softened but not coloured, about 6–8 minutes. Tip the rice into the pan, stir well to coat and cook for about 2 minutes until the rice starts to turn translucent. Pour in the remaining wine and let bubble until all the liquid has been absorbed. Add a ladleful of hot stock and stir until it is all absorbed. Continue adding the stock in this way, a ladleful at a time, until the rice is creamy with a slight bite. (You may not need all the stock.)

Stir the prawns and squid into the risotto and simmer for 2 minutes until they are just cooked through, adding the mussels for the last minute. Finally, stir in the grated lemon zest and remaining butter and taste for seasoning. Take the pan off the heat and leave to stand for a few minutes.

Divide the risotto between warm serving bowls and sprinkle with the chopped parsley. Serve at once.

Stuffed red mullet
with roasted new potatoes

THIS IS A GREAT WAY TO SAVOUR RED MULLET, a popular fish around the Mediterranean. Get your fishmonger to scale, gut and butterfly the red mullet, leaving the tails intact. This way, you can neatly stuff each fish with the tasty black olive and anchovy paste. Depending on the size of the fish, you may have some paste left over – keep it in a jar in the fridge and use to flavour other fish or chicken dishes.

SERVES 4

4 red mullet, about 500g each, butterflied
200g black olives, pitted
4 anchovy fillets in oil, drained
60g sun-dried tomatoes
2 garlic cloves, peeled and roughly chopped
5 tbsp olive oil, plus extra to oil
sea salt and black pepper

Roasted potatoes:
1kg small new potatoes, halved
2 lemons, cut into small wedges
few rosemary sprigs, leaves stripped
6 garlic cloves, with skin on
3 tbsp olive oil

First, roast the new potatoes. Preheat the oven to 200°C/Fan 180°C/Gas 6. Tip the potatoes, lemons, rosemary, garlic and olive oil into a large baking dish. Season with salt and pepper and toss well. Roast in the oven for about an hour until the potatoes are crisp on the outside and soft and fluffy in the middle.

About 20 minutes before the potatoes will be ready, rinse the fish cavities and carefully pat dry. Put the olives, anchovies, sun-dried tomatoes, garlic and 2 tbsp of the olive oil into a blender and blitz to a wet paste.

Generously stuff the fish cavities with the olive and anchovy paste, then rub the remaining olive oil all over the skins and season with salt and pepper. Lay the fish on a lightly oiled baking tray and roast in the oven for 15–20 minutes, depending on their thickness, until just cooked through – they should feel just firm when lightly pressed.

Divide the roasted potatoes between warm plates and place a stuffed red mullet alongside. Serve a lightly dressed green salad on the side.

Pappardelle with rabbit ragù

EMILIA-ROMAGNA IS HOME to some of the finest Italian cooking, not least this wonderfully tasty rabbit dish. I'm using farmed rabbit here, for its tender meat, but you can use a wild one for a stronger, gamier flavour if you prefer, allowing an extra 15–20 minutes braising time. You should be able to buy fresh pappardelle from a good Italian deli – or, of course, you can make your own. Otherwise, use good dried pasta.

SERVES 4

3 tbsp olive oil

1 farmed rabbit, jointed into 8 pieces

sea salt and black pepper

3 garlic cloves, peeled and chopped

2 onions, peeled and chopped

1 fennel bulb, trimmed and chopped

1 carrot, peeled and chopped

75g pancetta, diced

1 tbsp juniper berries, lightly crushed

2 rosemary sprigs, leaves picked and finely chopped

2 thyme sprigs, leaves picked

250ml red wine

2 tbsp tomato purée

300ml chicken stock

1 tbsp grainy mustard

500g fresh pappardelle or tagliatelle

handful of flat-leaf parsley, leaves roughly chopped

freshly grated Parmesan, to serve

Heat the olive oil in a large, wide heavy-based pan. Season the rabbit pieces with salt and pepper and fry them for 2 minutes on each side until browned. Remove with a slotted spoon to a plate.

Add the garlic, onions, fennel and carrot to the pan. Fry over a high heat for 2–3 minutes until slightly softened, then add the pancetta and continue to fry until it is lightly browned, about 6–8 minutes.

Add the juniper berries, rosemary and thyme, then return the browned rabbit pieces to the pan. Add the wine and tomato purée and let bubble until the liquid has reduced by half. Stir in the stock, season and put the lid on. Cook for 20–30 minutes until the rabbit is tender.

Take out the rabbit pieces and place on a board. When cool enough to handle, remove the meat from the bones, shredding larger pieces as necessary. If the sauce is very thin, simmer it until thickened to a light coating consistency. Return the rabbit meat to the sauce and heat through. Stir in the mustard, taste and adjust the seasoning.

When almost ready to serve, bring a large saucepan of salted water to the boil. Add the pasta and cook for a few minutes until al dente. Drain well and toss with the rabbit ragù, making sure the pasta is nicely coated with the sauce.

Divide between warm serving plates and spoon over any remaining ragù. Scatter over some parsley leaves and serve with grated Parmesan for sprinkling over.

Osso buco with roasted butternut squash and creamy polenta

LITERALLY MEANING 'HOLE IN THE BONE', this classic dish of braised veal shanks hails from Milan. Many insist that the original version did not include tomatoes, but over the years they have been introduced, creating a distinctive brownish red sauce. When ordering the veal, inform your butcher that you are making osso buco so he can supply you with the proper cut of veal shin.

SERVES 4

4 large pieces veal shin (bone-in),
   4–5cm thick
25g plain flour
sea salt and black pepper
3 tbsp olive oil
2 onions, peeled and chopped
3 garlic cloves, peeled and sliced
200ml dry white wine
3 thyme sprigs
3 rosemary sprigs
1 bay leaf
225ml passata
250ml chicken stock
handful of flat-leaf parsley leaves

Roasted butternut squash:
1 large butternut squash
2–3 tbsp olive oil
2 garlic cloves, peeled and sliced
2 thyme or rosemary sprigs,
   leaves stripped

Creamy polenta:
100g instant polenta
750ml water
20g butter
30g Parmesan, freshly grated
1 tbsp mascarpone
squeeze of lemon juice, to taste

Preheat the oven to 200°C/Fan 180°C/Gas 6. Lay the veal pieces on a board. Season the flour with salt and pepper and use to lightly coat the veal. Heat the olive oil in a large, wide heavy-based pan or flameproof casserole and brown the veal pieces in batches, turning them to colour all over; set aside on a plate.

Add the onions to the pan and fry gently for 2–3 minutes, then add the garlic. Cook until the onions are soft and lightly golden, then pour in the wine and add the thyme, rosemary and bay leaf. Let bubble until the liquid has reduced by two-thirds. Stir in the passata, season with salt and pepper and cook for 2–3 minutes. Pour in the stock, cover with a lid and cook in the oven for 1^{1}/$_{2}$ hours, turning the meat halfway through cooking.

Meanwhile, peel and deseed the squash, then cut into small chunks. Place in a large bowl with the olive oil, garlic, thyme or rosemary and some salt and pepper. Toss well, then transfer to a baking tray. When the osso buco has been cooking for about 50 minutes, place the tray of squash in the oven and roast for about 40 minutes until tender.

In the meantime, prepare the polenta. Pour the water into a large pan, add a pinch of salt and bring to the boil. Slowly whisk in the polenta and keep stirring for about 5 minutes until it thickens and has absorbed all of the water. Remove from the heat and stir in the butter, Parmesan, mascarpone and lemon juice to taste. Season with pepper and a little more salt to taste, if needed. Keep warm until ready to serve.

Discard the thyme, rosemary and bay leaf from the osso buco. Pile the creamy polenta onto warm plates and top with the osso buco. Finish with a sprinkling of parsley and serve the roasted squash alongside.

Caramelised peaches with **vin santo**

PEACHES ARE OFTEN PAIRED WITH WINE in Italy – as an aperitif, I am partial to a peach bellini. I also enjoy them baked with a traditional almondy stuffing and served topped with a prosecco-flavoured zabaglione. Here is an effortless way to transform ripe peaches into a lovely dessert. If you don't have any vin santo, use a sweet Marsala wine or a splash of Amaretto liqueur, whatever you have to hand.

SERVES 4

100g granulated or caster sugar
3 tbsp water
1 vanilla pod, slit open
100ml vin santo
50g unsalted butter, softened
8 firm but ripe peaches, stoned and quartered
good-quality vanilla ice cream, to serve

Put the sugar and water into a medium heavy-based saucepan (that will hold the peaches) over a medium-low heat. Once the sugar has dissolved, increase the heat and cook the syrup to a light caramel colour. Remove from the heat. Scrape the seeds from the vanilla pod directly into the pan and stir in the vin santo and butter.

Return the pan to a medium heat and stir the sauce until it is smooth. Add the peaches and cook for a few minutes until they have softened slightly but are still holding their shape. Take the pan off the heat.

Divide the peaches and sauce between serving bowls and top each one with a generous scoop of very cold vanilla ice cream. Serve at once.

Marsala roasted figs
with zabaglione

RIPE, JUICY FIGS IN SEASON are transformed to an elegant dessert with this simple recipe. The figs acquire additional sweetness and a sophisticated depth of flavour from the Marsala.

SERVES 4

softened butter, for greasing
8 ripe figs
3 tbsp Marsala wine
50g soft brown sugar
grated zest and juice of $1/2$ orange
handful of pistachio nuts, toasted
    and chopped

Zabaglione:
4 large egg yolks
60g icing sugar, sifted
finely grated zest of 1 lemon
75ml Marsala wine

Preheat the oven to 150°C/Fan 130°C/Gas 2. Generously butter a shallow ovenproof dish large enough to hold the figs. Trim the stalks, then slash the top of each fig in a criss-cross fashion and gently squeeze the base to open the fruit slightly. Stand the figs in the buttered dish.

In a small bowl, mix together the Marsala, brown sugar, orange zest and juice. Spoon this mixture over the figs and roast in the oven for 10 minutes. Take out the dish and baste the figs with the pan juices, then return to the oven for a further 5 minutes.

To make the zabaglione, put the egg yolks and icing sugar into a large heatproof bowl and set over a pan of barely simmering water. Using a hand-held electric whisk, slowly and steadily whisk the mixture until it turns pale, thick and creamy; take care to avoid overheating. At this point, increase the whisking speed. Add the lemon zest and then gradually whisk in the Marsala. Continue to whisk for a further 10 minutes or so, until the zabaglione is thick and foamy, and the mixture leaves a trail when the beaters are lifted above the surface. Take the bowl off the pan and leave the zabaglione to cool slightly, whisking occasionally.

To serve, spoon the zabaglione over the roasted figs and sprinkle with the chopped pistachios. Serve while still warm.

Amaretto and **chocolate torte**

THIS IRRESISTIBLE CHOCOLATE TORTE has a rich, melt-in-the-mouth texture. It makes a fantastic dessert for entertaining because you can cook it ahead of time and keep it chilled – just remember to take it out of the fridge about 30 minutes before serving to enjoy it at its best.

SERVES 8

softened butter, for greasing
350g dark chocolate
    (about 60% cocoa solids)
6 tbsp Amaretto di Saronno
    liqueur
4 large eggs, separated
50g amaretti biscuits, finely
    crushed
200g caster sugar
cocoa powder, to dust
lightly whipped cream or
    mascarpone, to serve

Preheat the oven to 180°C/Fan 160°C/Gas 4. Butter a 20cm round cake tin with removable base and line the base with greaseproof paper.

Break the chocolate into pieces, place in a heatproof bowl and set over a pan of barely simmering water. As it begins to melt, stir in the liqueur. When the chocolate has completely melted and is smooth, remove from the heat and set aside to cool slightly.

Beat the egg yolks together in large bowl until thick and creamy. Mix the crushed amaretti into the chocolate mixture, then stir in the egg yolks.

In a separate clean bowl, whisk the egg whites to soft peaks using a hand-held electric whisk. Now whisk in the caster sugar, a tablespoonful at a time, until you have a firm glossy meringue. Fold the egg whites into the chocolate mixture, a third at a time.

Spoon the mixture into the prepared tin and gently smooth the surface. Bake in the oven for 35–40 minutes until the torte is risen and the top is slightly crusty. The surface may crack, but the middle should be lovely and moist. Turn off the oven and leave the torte to cool slowly inside for at least an hour.

Remove the torte from the oven and allow to cool completely before unmoulding. Transfer to a large serving plate and dust with cocoa powder. Serve, cut into slices, with lightly whipped cream or mascarpone.

GREEK

GREEK FOOD IS OFTEN UNDERESTIMATED AND CAN
BE QUITE DELICIOUS. ESSENTIALLY A SIMPLE STYLE
OF COOKING, IT DRAWS CLOSELY FROM WHAT IS GROWN
LOCALLY AND FISHED FROM THE SEA. HERBS SUCH AS
ROSEMARY AND OREGANO GROW EVERYWHERE IN THE
HILLS AND ARE USED ABUNDANTLY, AND THE BEES
THAT FEED OFF THE POLLEN MAKE DELECTABLE
HONEY, WHICH ALSO FEATURES STRONGLY IN COOKING.
FETA IS THE MOST COMMONLY USED CHEESE AND
I LOVE THE CRUMBLY TEXTURE AND LOVELY SALTINESS
IT LENDS A DISH. MOST OF US PROBABLY THINK OF
MOUSSAKA AS THE MOST TYPICAL GREEK DISH AND
I'VE INCLUDED A RECIPE FOR IT HERE, BUT THERE'S
MORE TO GREEK FOOD... IT'S NOT ALL ABOUT KEBABS.

Taramasalata with home-made pitta

A STAPLE GREEK MEZE DISH, taramasalata is easy to buy, but commercially produced taramasalata – invariably tainted pink with food colouring – tastes nothing like the real thing. Pure, home-made taramasalata has an intense flavour of smoked cod's roe, which can be mellowed by adjusting the amount of olive oil. At the restaurants, we make our dip with a hefty amount of good olive oil to get a very smooth, creamy texture – much like a thick mayonnaise.

SERVES 6

2½ thick slices of white bread, crusts removed
100ml whole milk
200g smoked cod's roe
1 garlic clove, peeled and crushed
juice of 1½ lemons
sea salt and black pepper
275ml light olive oil
a little milk (if needed)
extra virgin olive oil, to drizzle

Pitta bread:
450g strong white flour, plus extra to dust
1 tsp fine sea salt
2 x 7g sachets fast-action dry yeast
1 tbsp extra virgin olive oil, plus extra to oil the bowl
300ml tepid water

First, make the pitta dough. Mix the flour, salt and yeast together in a large bowl. Make a well in the centre and pour in the extra virgin olive oil and most of the water. Stir to bring the mixture together into a ball, adding a little more water as necessary to get a soft, but not sticky, dough. Tip out onto a lightly floured surface and knead for 10 minutes until smooth. Put the dough in a lightly oiled clean bowl, cover with cling film and leave to rise in a warm place for about 2 hours.

To make the taramasalata, tear the bread into small pieces, place in a bowl, pour over the milk and set aside to soak. Cut away any hard bits of skin from the cod's roe, then place the roe in a food processor along with the garlic, lemon juice and a good grinding of pepper. Add the soaked bread and blend to a smooth paste. With the motor running, gradually trickle in the light olive oil through the funnel. Taste and adjust the seasoning with salt and pepper and add a touch more milk if the taramasalata seems too oily. Spoon into a bowl.

When the pitta dough has roughly doubled in size, punch it down and knead briefly on a lightly floured surface for a minute. Divide into 12 equal pieces and shape into balls. Leave to prove in a warm place for 15 minutes. Meanwhile, preheat the oven to 200°C/Fan 180°C/Gas 6 and put 2 lightly oiled baking trays inside to heat. Roll each dough ball out into an oval, 2–3mm thick. Transfer to the warmed baking trays and bake in the oven for 6–8 minutes until puffed up and light golden in colour.

Drizzle a little extra virgin olive oil over the surface of the taramasalata before serving, with the warm pitta breads.

Griddled haloumi and **aubergine** salad

HALOUMI IS A CYPRIOT CHEESE traditionally made from a combination of goat's and ewe's milk. However, many commercial varieties now include cow's milk, which produces an inferior cheese. Do try to get hold of an authentic haloumi – the flavour and texture will make all the difference to this lovely salad. If you have any olive dressing left over, keep it in a jar in the fridge to use for drizzling over grilled fish or lamb.

SERVES 6

1 large aubergine
sea salt and black pepper
6 ripe plum tomatoes
40g Kalamata olives, pitted
small bunch of mint, leaves
   shredded
olive oil, for brushing
500g haloumi
2–3 tbsp plain flour

Olive dressing:
75g Kalamata olives, pitted
3 tbsp red wine vinegar
1 tsp dried oregano
75ml olive oil
75ml groundnut oil

Cut the aubergine into thin slices. Place in a colander, sprinkle lightly with salt and leave to stand for 20 minutes. (The salt will help to draw out excess moisture from the aubergine.) Pat dry with kitchen paper.

Cut the tomatoes into wedges and put into a large bowl with the olives and mint. Set aside while you make the dressing.

For the dressing, tip the olives, wine vinegar and dried oregano into a blender and blitz to a smooth purée. With the motor running, gradually pour in the olive and groundnut oils and season well with salt and pepper to taste. Transfer to a jar and set aside.

About 15 minutes before you will be ready to serve, put a griddle pan over a high heat. Brush the aubergine slices with olive oil and griddle for about 2 minutes on each side until softened and slightly charred. Add to the bowl of tomatoes, pour over some of the dressing and toss to coat.

Thinly slice the haloumi and lightly coat with flour. Griddle the slices until they are turning golden brown around the edges and just starting to melt.

To serve, arrange the griddled aubergine on a large platter and top with the haloumi. Spoon the tomato and olive salad on top and drizzle over a little more olive dressing. Serve at once, while the haloumi is still warm.

White bean and vegetable soup

KNOWN AS *FASOULADA* IN GREECE, this is a wonderfully sustaining and economical soup. It's very easy to prepare – you just need to remember to put the beans to soak the night before, and allow for a couple of hours simmering on the hob. Serve with country bread as a wholesome lunch, or in small bowls as a rustic starter.

SERVES 4–6

500g dried white beans, such as haricot beans or Greek *fasolia gigantes*, soaked overnight in plenty of cold water
3–4 tbsp olive oil
2 carrots, peeled and finely chopped
1 large onion, peeled and finely chopped
2 celery sticks, peeled and finely chopped
2 garlic cloves, peeled and finely chopped
sea salt and black pepper
6 ripe plum tomatoes, skinned, deseeded and finely chopped
1 tbsp tomato purée
1 tsp dried oregano
small handful of flat-leaf parsley, leaves chopped

To serve (optional):
extra virgin olive oil, to drizzle
crumbled feta, to finish

Drain the white beans, tip into a large saucepan and pour over fresh cold water to cover generously. Bring to the boil over a medium heat and skim off the scum and froth from the surface. Lower the heat and simmer for about an hour.

Heat the olive oil in another saucepan. Add the carrots, onion, celery, garlic and some seasoning. Cook, stirring frequently, over a medium-high heat for 6–8 minutes until the vegetables begin to soften. Add the chopped tomatoes, tomato purée and dried oregano. Stir over the heat for another minute or two, then tip the contents of the pan into the pot of beans.

Add a little more water if necessary to ensure that everything is covered and simmer for another 30–45 minutes until the beans are soft. If the soup becomes too thick, dilute it with a splash of hot water.

To serve, ladle the soup into warm bowls and scatter over the chopped parsley. If you wish, drizzle each bowl with a little extra virgin olive oil and top with the some crumbled feta. Serve hot.

Barbecuing sardines

Sardines take on a lovely smoky flavour on the barbecue, so I'll invariably opt to cook them this way if I possibly can. The secret to a successful barbecue is to make sure that the fire is not too hot when you put the food on the grill. The coals should be grey and ashen with a good heat rising above.

Barbecued sardines with **tzatziki**

TZATZIKI MAY BE A SURPRISING accompaniment to sardines, but I find it works well as the acidity from the lemon juice and yoghurt helps to counter the oiliness of the fish. Make it an hour or two in advance to allow time for the flavours to develop.

SERVES 4–6

12 very fresh sardines,
    scaled and gutted
olive oil, to drizzle
sea salt and black pepper

Tzatziki:
1 cucumber
2 garlic cloves, peeled and grated
350g Greek yoghurt
juice of 1/2 lemon, or to taste
2 tbsp extra virgin olive oil

To serve:
extra virgin olive oil, to drizzle
small handful of mint leaves,
    chopped

To prepare the tzatziki, peel the cucumber, cut in half lengthways and scrape out the seeds. Coarsely grate the flesh, sprinkle with 1 tsp salt and place in a sieve set over a bowl. Leave to drain for an hour or so, then squeeze out as much excess water from the flesh as possible, using your hands.

Mix the grated cucumber, garlic, yoghurt, lemon juice and extra virgin olive oil together in a bowl. Season with salt and pepper to taste, then cover and refrigerate.

Light the barbecue and wait for the fire to burn down to grey embers (see preceding pages). Or, if you are cooking indoors, heat a griddle pan until hot. Rinse the sardines and pat dry, then rub all over with a little olive oil and some salt and pepper. Place the sardines on the grill (or griddle) and cook for about 3 minutes on each side until the flesh feels firm, but still comes away from the bone easily.

Pile the hot sardines onto a platter and serve with the tzatziki on the side. Finish with a drizzle of extra virgin olive oil and a scattering of chopped mint.

Squid stuffed with tomato and herb rice

THIS IS A VERY TASTY ONE-POT DISH. Baby squid are stuffed with a mixture of rice, tomatoes, onions and fresh herbs and any extra stuffing is added to the pan to cook alongside. For a little touch of sweetness and extra texture, add a handful of raisins and pine nuts to the rice mixture. You can also throw a couple of chopped tomatoes into the sauce to give it a little acidity.

SERVES 5

10 baby squid, cleaned, tentacles
    reserved
olive oil, to drizzle

Rice stuffing:
2 tbsp olive oil
1 red onion, peeled and finely
    chopped
2 garlic cloves, peeled and finely
    chopped
100ml dry white wine
300g long-grain white rice
4 plum tomatoes, skinned,
    deseeded and diced
1 tsp caster sugar
sea salt and black pepper
850ml water
handful of mint, leaves chopped
handful of flat-leaf parsley, leaves
    chopped, plus extra to finish

First, prepare the stuffing. Heat the olive oil in a wide pan over a medium heat and add the onion and garlic. Sauté gently for 6–8 minutes until softened but not coloured. Increase the heat slightly and pour in the wine. Let bubble until the liquid has reduced by half, then add the rice to the pan and cook for a minute, stirring continuously.

Next, add the tomatoes, sugar and some salt and pepper. Pour in 600ml water, then cover with a lid and leave to simmer for 12–15 minutes, or until the water has been absorbed and the rice is fluffy. Remove from the heat and leave to stand for 5 minutes. Fluff up the rice with a fork, then allow to cool, before stirring in the chopped mint and parsley.

Preheat the oven to 180°C/Fan 160°C/Gas 4. Carefully stuff the squid pouches with the rice mixture and thread a cocktail stick through the top of each one to hold in the stuffing. Lay the stuffed squid in an oiled ovenproof dish.

Add the tentacles and any remaining rice stuffing to the dish and pour the remaining 250ml water over the top. Drizzle with a little olive oil. Bake in the oven for 30–35 minutes until the squid is tender and cooked through. Scatter over some chopped parsley to serve.

Moussaka

FOR MY VERSION OF THIS POPULAR DISH, the aubergine slices, meat sauce and cheese sauce are layered, then topped with a sprinkling of grated cheese, much like an Italian lasagne. Although not authentic, I find that the inclusion of grated Cheddar makes it all the more delicious.

SERVES 4

3–4 tbsp olive oil, plus extra
    for brushing
3 large onions, peeled and finely
    chopped
4 garlic cloves, peeled and finely
    chopped
1kg lean minced lamb
sea salt and black pepper
200ml red wine
4 tbsp tomato purée
2 x 400g tins chopped plum
    tomatoes
2 cinnamon sticks
1/2 tsp ground allspice
small handful of oregano, leaves
    finely chopped
2 large aubergines

Cheese sauce:
75g butter
75g plain flour
600ml whole milk
150g Cheddar, grated
2 medium eggs, beaten

Heat the olive oil in a large saucepan over a medium heat. Add the onions and garlic and fry until soft and light golden brown. Increase the heat slightly, add the mince with some seasoning and fry, stirring, until evenly browned. Pour in the wine and let bubble until it has almost all evaporated before adding the tomato purée, tomatoes, cinnamon, allspice and oregano. Simmer for 30–35 minutes, stirring occasionally.

Meanwhile, cut the aubergines into 1.5–2cm thick slices. Brush them generously with olive oil and sprinkle with a little salt and pepper. Place a frying pan over a high heat and fry the aubergine slices in batches, for 2 minutes on each side, until lightly browned.

Preheat the oven to 200°C/Fan 180°C/Gas 6. To make the sauce, melt the butter in a non-stick saucepan, add the flour and cook, stirring with a wooden spoon, for a minute or two. Lower the heat slightly and whisk in the milk, a little at a time. Allow to simmer gently for 8–10 minutes, then stir in 100g of the cheese and some seasoning. Remove from the heat, leave to cool slightly, then beat in the eggs.

Arrange a layer of aubergine slices in a deep 2 litre ovenproof dish, using a third of them. Discard the cinnamon sticks, then spoon half of the meat sauce over the aubergine layer. Spoon over a third of the cheese sauce. Repeat these layers, then cover with another layer of aubergine slices. Pour the remaining cheese sauce on top and sprinkle with the rest of the cheese. Bake in the oven for 35–45 minutes until the top is golden brown and bubbling. Let stand for 5 minutes or so before serving.

Lamb chops with avgolemono sauce

MARINATING LAMB CHOPS WITH OREGANO in a garlicky vinaigrette before grilling gives them a fantastic flavour – and pairing them with a lemony avgolemono sauce cuts through the richness of the meat. You can also serve this delicate sauce with vegetables and other grilled meats.

SERVES 4–6

12 lamb chops, about 180g each
150ml olive oil
75ml red wine vinegar
2 tsp dried oregano
4 garlic cloves, peeled and slightly crushed
sea salt and black pepper

Avgolemono sauce:
250ml chicken stock
3 large egg yolks
juice of 2 large lemons
few oregano sprigs, leaves chopped

Arrange the lamb chops in a single layer in a large ovenproof dish. In a bowl, whisk together the olive oil, wine vinegar, dried oregano, garlic and some salt and pepper. Pour this marinade over the lamb chops and turn them to coat all over. Cover the dish with cling film and leave to marinate in the fridge for 2–3 hours. Remove from the fridge 30 minutes before cooking to bring back to room temperature.

To make the avgolemono sauce, bring the stock to a gentle simmer in a saucepan over a low heat. Using a hand whisk, whisk the egg yolks in a large bowl until pale and frothy. Add the lemon juice and continue to whisk for a further minute. Slowly whisk this mixture into the warm stock. Be careful not to overheat or the sauce will curdle. Continue to whisk until the sauce thickens to a light coating consistency. Stir in the chopped oregano. Remove from the heat and season to taste. Pour into a warmed serving jug; keep warm.

Meanwhile, preheat the grill to its highest setting. Uncover the chops and grill them for 15–20 minutes, depending on thickness, turning them halfway through cooking. For medium-rare meat, the chops should feel slightly firm when pressed.

Serve the lamb chops immediately, with the avgolemono sauce and vegetables of your choice.

Spanakopita

THIS SPINACH AND FETA PIE is probably the most popular of all Greek pies, which are everyday fare in Greece and typically eaten as substantial snacks. I prefer to serve this scrumptious pie as a main course, or as a side dish to roast lamb.

SERVES 4

2 tbsp olive oil
2 large sweet onions, peeled and finely chopped
sea salt and black pepper
500g spinach leaves, washed and drained
nutmeg, to grate
250g feta, crumbled
2 large eggs
200ml double cream
50g pine nuts, toasted
100g butter, melted
14 sheets of filo pastry

Heat the olive oil in a frying pan over a medium heat and add the onions with a little salt and pepper. Fry, stirring frequently, for 6–8 minutes until soft but not coloured. Transfer to a large bowl.

Wilt the spinach leaves in several batches: stir them in a large saucepan over a medium-high heat until just wilted, then tip into a colander. Press down on the spinach with the back of a ladle to squeeze out as much excess water as possible. Allow to cool slightly, then chop roughly.

Add the spinach to the onion and grate over a little nutmeg. Add the feta, eggs and cream. Season with a generous grinding of pepper and just a small pinch of salt – as the feta is salty. Finally, stir in the pine nuts. Chill until ready to use.

Preheat the oven to 200°C/Fan 180°C/Gas 6. Brush the base of a large ovenproof dish with a little of the melted butter. Now layer 10 sheets of filo pastry in the dish, brushing each layer with butter and allowing any excess to overhang the sides. Spoon the spinach and feta mix over the pastry sheets and then fold any overhanging filo over the filling. Layer the remaining filo sheets on top, buttering generously and scrunching for an attractive finish.

Bake in the oven for 50–60 minutes until the top of the pie is golden and the filling is set. To check, insert a small knife into the centre of the pie – the filling should not look too runny.

Leave to stand for at least 10 minutes before slicing. Serve the pie either warm or at room temperature.

Walnut cake

DRENCHED IN A FRAGRANT SPICE SYRUP as soon as it comes out of the oven, this classic cake is delectably moist. It is known as *karydopita* in Greece and is often made without any flour, although I find adding a little makes for a lighter cake. It is best served with a generous dollop of Greek yoghurt and some strong Greek tea or coffee to counteract the sweetness.

SERVES 4

softened butter, for greasing
5 large eggs, separated
2 tbsp brandy
grated zest and juice of 1 orange
90g caster sugar
1/2 tsp ground cinnamon
1/4 tsp ground cloves
20g self-raising flour, sifted
2 tsp baking powder
35g day-old white breadcrumbs
175g walnut pieces

Spice syrup:
125g caster sugar
150ml water
3 cloves
1 cinnamon stick
juice and thinly pared zest of
    1 lemon

Preheat the oven to 190°C/Fan 170°C/Gas 5. Butter and line the base and sides of a 23cm cake tin, preferably with a removable base.

In a large bowl, beat together the egg yolks, brandy, orange zest and juice until smooth and creamy.

Put the sugar, cinnamon, cloves, flour, baking powder, breadcrumbs and 150g of the walnuts into a food processor and blitz to fine crumbs. Tip the mixture into a large mixing bowl. In a separate, clean bowl, whisk the egg whites to firm peaks.

Fold the egg yolk mixture into the crumb mixture, then carefully fold in the egg whites, using a large metal spoon, until evenly incorporated.

Pour the cake mixture into the prepared tin and bake in the oven for 40 minutes. To test, insert a skewer into the centre – if it comes out clean then the cake is done, if not return to the oven for a few more minutes.

Make the spice syrup while the cake is in the oven. Put all the ingredients into a small saucepan and stir over a medium heat until the sugar is dissolved. Bring to the boil and then simmer for 5 minutes. Leave to cool completely before straining through a sieve into a jug. Chop or crush the remaining walnuts into small pieces.

Once the cake is ready, remove from the oven and prick all over with a thin skewer. Sprinkle over the remaining walnuts, then spoon the cold syrup over the hot cake. Allow to cool before unmoulding and serving.

Pan-fried **watermelon** with **yoghurt** and caramelised **walnuts**

SWEET, JUICY WATERMELONS ARE MUCH LOVED by the Greeks. When this refreshing fruit is at its peak towards the end of August, it often appears at breakfast, with feta and olives in lunchtime salads, and, of course, as a dessert. I like to pan-fry watermelon slices to bring out their natural sweetness – and serve them topped with honey caramelised walnuts and thick yoghurt for a tempting dessert.

SERVES 4

1 small or $^1/_2$ medium watermelon
a little olive oil
icing sugar, to dust
400–500g Greek yoghurt

Caramelised walnuts:
15g butter
65g runny honey
100g walnuts

To prepare the caramelised walnuts, line a baking tray with greaseproof paper. Put the butter and honey into a small heavy-based saucepan and place over a medium heat for 2–3 minutes until the butter has melted. Now add the walnuts, stirring to coat well. Continue to heat for a further minute or two until the mixture starts to bubble and turn golden brown. Carefully tip onto the lined baking tray and set aside for 1–2 hours until set. (Don't expect the caramelised nuts to be brittle like praline, as they have a softer set.) Break into small pieces with your hands and store in an airtight container until needed.

When you are almost ready to serve, cut the watermelon into 3–4cm thick triangles or squares. Heat a little olive oil in a non-stick frying pan over a high heat. You will need to pan-fry the watermelon in batches. Dust the slices on both sides with icing sugar, then fry for 1–1$^1/_2$ minutes on each side. Remove to a warm plate and repeat with the rest.

Place a pan-fried watermelon slice on each plate, add a generous dollop of yoghurt and scatter over the caramelised walnuts. Serve at once.

SPANISH

I LOVE GOING TO SPAIN AND I'VE SPENT A LOT OF TIME
IN SAN SEBASTIÁN. ARZAK, THE RENOWNED FAMILY-
RUN RESTAURANT IN THE CITY, IS ONE OF THE FEW
WHERE A FEMALE CHEF HOLDS 3 MICHELIN STARS.
CATALONIA, OF COURSE, IS THE HOME OF FERRAN
ADRIÀ'S FAMOUS EL BULLI RESTAURANT, WHERE THE
FOOD NEVER CEASES TO AMAZE ME. BUT WHAT REALLY
DRAWS ME TO SPANISH FOOD IS THE SIMPLE RUSTIC
PLEASURES – A GREAT PAELLA OR SOME SIMPLY
COOKED FISH OR SHELLFISH, PERHAPS. AND I ADORE
THE SPANISH TAPAS CUSTOM. IT WAS THE INSPIRATION
FOR OUR MAZE RESTAURANT, WHERE SMALL PLATES
ARE SERVED, SO YOU CAN ENJOY A DINNER COMPRISING
LOTS OF DIFFERENT DISHES.

Chilled almond and garlic soup
with grapes

A MOORISH TAKE ON GAZPACHO, whereby blanched almonds, garlic and white bread take the place of fresh tomatoes and vegetables. A handful of grapes and toasted almonds added to each bowl contrasts and balances the delicate creaminess of the soup.

SERVES 4

200g good rustic white bread
150g blanched almonds
1 large garlic clove, peeled and roughly chopped
200ml good-quality extra virgin olive oil, plus extra to drizzle (optional)
1^1/$_2$–2 tbsp sherry vinegar
350–400ml ice-cold water

To serve:
150–200g white seedless grapes, halved
2 tbsp flaked or nibbed almonds, toasted
handful of ice cubes (optional)

Remove the crusts from the bread, then cut it into cubes and place in a bowl. Pour over enough cold water to just cover, leave to soak for 2–3 minutes, then squeeze out the excess water from the bread.

Put the bread into a food processor or blender. Add the almonds, garlic, olive oil and sherry vinegar and blend until smooth. With the motor running, slowly pour in the ice-cold water until the soup is the thickness of double cream. If you prefer it thinner, add a little more water. Pour the soup into a bowl, cover and refrigerate until well chilled.

To serve, ladle the soup into chilled bowls and arrange the halved grapes and toasted almonds on top. If you wish, add an ice cube to each bowl and drizzle over a little extra virgin olive oil before serving.

Garlic **prawns**

OF CATALAN ORIGIN, THIS SIMPLE TAPAS dish is now served all over Spain. Use very fresh prawns to ensure a sweet, succulent result. Eat them with your fingers and don't forget to provide a bowl for the empty prawn shells and individual bowls of lemon water for rinsing sticky fingers.

SERVES 4

600g large raw prawns
4 tbsp olive oil
5–6 garlic cloves, peeled and
    thinly sliced
2 dried red chillies, finely chopped
sea salt and black pepper

To serve:
a few flat-leaf parsley leaves,
    chopped
lemon wedges

Either leave the prawns in their shells, or if you prefer, remove the heads, peel and devein, leaving the tails intact.

Heat the olive oil in a large frying pan. Add the garlic, dried chillies and a pinch each of salt and pepper. Fry over a medium-low heat for about a minute until the garlic begins to colour very slightly. Immediately tip the prawns into the pan, increase the heat and fry for about $1\frac{1}{2}$ minutes on each side until bright red and opaque.

Arrange the prawns on a warm platter or individual plates, drizzle over the garlic-infused oil from the pan and sprinkle with a little chopped parsley. Serve immediately, with lemon wedges. Accompany with plenty of crusty bread.

Broad beans
with Iberico **ham**

THIS IS A CLASSIC SPANISH COMBINATION and one of the easiest tapas to assemble. I recommend using Iberico ham as its superb, slightly nutty flavour is second to none – you should be able to get it from a good deli.

SERVES 4

500g broad beans (ideally freshly podded,
    otherwise frozen and thawed)
sea salt and black pepper
3 tbsp olive oil
100g Iberico ham, diced
1 onion, peeled and finely chopped
2 garlic cloves, peeled and finely chopped
1 tbsp chopped flat-leaf parsley

Add the broad beans to a pan of boiling salted water, bring back to the boil and blanch for 2–3 minutes until only just tender. Drain in a colander and place under cold running water to refresh, then drain again.

Heat the olive oil in a frying pan. Add the ham and fry, stirring, for 2–3 minutes. Add the onion and garlic and fry gently for 6–8 minutes until softened but not coloured. Tip the blanched broad beans into the pan and toss over the heat for 2–3 minutes, seasoning well with salt and pepper to taste.

Transfer the broad beans and ham to a warm bowl, sprinkle with chopped parsley and accompany with toasted slices of rustic bread.

Tortilla

THE RENOWNED TORTILLA HAS ATTAINED the title of national dish – the *tortilla Espanola*. Different kinds of tortilla exist all over Spain – in Valencia they are often made with rice and ham, whereas in Granada the popular *tortilla del Sacromonte* is made with bull's testicles and cow's brains. The following simple recipe is based on a typical Madrid-style tortilla.

SERVES 8

900g medium floury potatoes, such as Maris Piper
100ml olive oil
1 large onion, peeled and thinly sliced
sea salt and black pepper
6 large eggs

Peel the potatoes and cut them into thin slices. Heat the olive oil in a large, wide heavy-based pan. Add the potatoes and onion with some seasoning and toss well to coat in the oil. Reduce the heat and fry the potatoes for 15–20 minutes, stirring occasionally to prevent them from sticking to the bottom of the pan.

When the potatoes and onions are soft but not browned, remove the pan from the heat and drain off the excess oil into a bowl; save this for later. Whisk the eggs lightly in a large bowl; do not overbeat. Fold the slightly cooled potatoes into the egg mixture and leave to rest for a few minutes.

Heat 2–3 tbsp of the reserved oil in a 25–26cm non-stick frying pan and pour in the potato and egg mixture, tilting the pan to spread it evenly over the base. Leave to cook gently for 4–6 minutes or until the base is a light golden brown colour and the tortilla begins to leave the sides of the pan.

Carefully flip the tortilla over and cook the other side. To do this, run a flexible heatproof spatula around the sides of the tortilla, then place an inverted plate on top of the pan and carefully turn both the pan and plate over. Using the spatula, slide the tortilla back into the pan so that the browned side is facing upwards. Cook for a few more minutes until the underside is cooked; allow less time if you prefer the middle to be moist and slightly runny.

Carefully slide the tortilla onto a serving plate and allow to cool – it is best eaten at room temperature. Serve cut into wedges as a tapa, or alongside a mixed salad for a tasty lunch.

Paella with chicken and chorizo

ORIGINALLY FROM VALENCIA, paella is now cooked in every region of Spain. There are hundreds of different recipes, using just about any ingredient that works well with rice. *Paella Valenciana* traditionally includes chicken, rabbit and snails, whereas *paella marisco* (mixed seafood paella) is more common in the coastal areas. Do try to buy a proper paella rice, as it will soak up more of the saffron-infused stock than long-grain rice.

SERVES 4–6

400g medium-grain paella rice, such as Bomba or Calasparra
6 boneless, skinless chicken thighs, about 600g
sea salt and black pepper
250g raw chorizo sausage, skinned
3 tbsp olive oil
1 red pepper, cored, deseeded and chopped
1 green pepper, cored, deseeded and chopped
6 garlic cloves, peeled and finely chopped
125ml dry white wine
1 litre chicken stock
pinch of saffron strands
1/2 tsp paprika
100g peas, thawed if frozen
6 large tomatoes, skinned, deseeded and chopped
handful of flat-leaf parsley leaves, chopped
lemon wedges, to serve

Rinse the rice well, drain and set aside. Cut the chicken into bite-sized pieces and season with salt and pepper. Cut the chorizo sausage into thick slices.

Heat the olive oil in a large sauté pan – or a paella pan if you have one – and brown the chicken pieces all over; remove to a plate and set aside. Add the chorizo slices to the pan and sauté for 2 minutes, then add the chopped peppers and garlic. Cook for 3–4 minutes, stirring frequently, until the peppers start to soften.

Stir in the rice and cook, stirring, for a few minutes to toast the grains. Pour in the wine and let it bubble until reduced by half. Now add the stock, saffron and paprika. Bring to the boil, then return the chicken pieces to the pan and lower the heat. Simmer for 15 minutes, stirring every so often.

Add the peas and chopped tomatoes and continue cooking, very gently, for a further 10 minutes, stirring every once in a while. When the rice is just cooked but still retains a slight bite, remove the pan from the heat and leave to stand for a few minutes.

Scatter the chopped parsley over the paella, then bring to the table and serve with lemon wedges.

Basque hake
and **potato** casserole

KNOWN AS MERLUZA, Basque hake is a dark-skinned fish with very tasty, firm flesh. It is considered a delicacy locally and can be quite expensive when caught from the Bay of Biscay. Merluza has become increasingly scarce so when I make this dish at home, I use the more sustainable South African Cape hake.

SERVES 4

750g hake fillets
4 garlic cloves, peeled
5 tbsp olive oil
1 tbsp sweet paprika
125ml dry white wine
1 large onion, peeled and thinly
    sliced
500g new potatoes, peeled and
    quartered
sea salt and black pepper
200g peas, thawed if frozen

Check the hake for small bones, removing any with kitchen tweezers, then cut the fish into 5cm pieces and set aside. Thinly slice two of the garlic cloves. Heat 3 tbsp olive oil in a frying pan, add the sliced garlic and fry gently until lightly golden. Remove from the heat and let the oil cool slightly before stirring in the paprika, followed by the wine. Set aside to infuse while you prepare the rest of the dish.

Cut the remaining 2 garlic cloves into quarters. Put the onion, potatoes, garlic quarters and remaining olive oil into a flameproof casserole. Add the garlic and paprika-infused wine and just enough water to cover. Season with salt and pepper and bring to the boil. Cook at a fast simmer for about 8–10 minutes, then add the hake pieces along with the peas. Lower the heat and cook at a gentle simmer for 3–5 minutes until both the potato and hake are just cooked. Taste and adjust the seasoning.

Ladle into warm bowls and serve at once, with plenty of rustic bread for mopping up the tasty juices.

Cod with romesco sauce

ROMESCO HAILS FROM CATALONIA, where it is frequently served as a sauce or a dip. Here, I'm baking cod fillets in a generous layer of romesco. It's a simple, healthy and tasty way to cook any variety of white fish.

SERVES 4

4 thick cod fillets, with skin, about 175g each
3 tbsp olive oil
100g blanched almonds
3–4 garlic cloves, peeled and thinly sliced
1 onion, peeled and finely chopped
pinch of dried chilli flakes, to taste
6 ripe beef tomatoes, skinned and finely chopped
1 bay leaf
sea salt and black pepper
85g good-quality white bread (about 2 slices), toasted and roughly chopped
2 tbsp chopped flat-leaf parsley, plus extra to finish
3–4 tbsp water
3 tbsp sherry vinegar

Check the cod fillets for pin-bones and pull out any that you come across with kitchen tweezers. Chill until ready to cook.

Preheat the oven to 180°C/Fan 160°C/Gas 4. Heat the olive oil in a large frying pan, add the almonds and garlic and fry gently until lightly golden. Remove from the pan with a slotted spoon and set aside on a plate.

Add the onion to the pan and fry gently until lightly golden. Add the dried chilli flakes, tomatoes and bay leaf. Stir well and season with salt and pepper. Simmer for 10 minutes or so, until the tomatoes are soft.

Meanwhile, put the almonds and garlic, bread and parsley into a blender or food processor with 1 tbsp water. Blend to a rough paste and then stir into the tomato mixture, along with another 2–3 tbsp water. Add the sherry vinegar, then taste and adjust the seasoning if necessary.

Arrange the cod fillets in an ovenproof dish, pour over the romesco sauce, cover the dish loosely with foil and bake in the oven for 15–20 minutes, depending upon the thickness of the fish, until it is just done. Serve straight from the dish, sprinkled with a little chopped parsley.

Meatballs in tomato sauce

SPANISH MEATBALLS, OR *ALBONDIGAS*, are commonly
served as tapas in bars across Spain. They also make a fantastic main
course – served with steamed rice or eaten simply with rustic bread
to mop up the sauce.

SERVES 4–5

Spanish meatballs:

500g good-quality minced beef
1 onion, peeled and very finely
    chopped
1 garlic clove, peeled and finely
    chopped
50g white breadcrumbs
25g Manchego (or Cheddar),
    grated
2 tbsp chopped flat-leaf parsley,
    plus extra to finish
sea salt and black pepper
1 large egg, lightly beaten
2 tbsp olive oil

Tomato sauce:

2 tbsp olive oil
1 onion, peeled and very finely
    chopped
1 garlic clove, peeled and finely
    chopped
120ml dry white wine
2 x 400g tins chopped tomatoes
100ml water
1–2 tsp caster sugar

To make the meatballs, mix the minced beef, onion, garlic, breadcrumbs, cheese and chopped parsley together in a large bowl until evenly combined. Season well with salt and pepper and add the beaten egg to bind, mixing with your hands. Break off a small piece of the mixture, shape into a ball and fry in an oiled pan until cooked, then taste for seasoning. Adjust the seasoning of the uncooked mixture as necessary.

With damp hands, shape the mixture into about 16 meatballs, trying not to press them too tightly. Place on a large plate, cover with cling film and chill for at least 30 minutes to allow them to firm up.

Meanwhile, make the tomato sauce. Heat the olive oil in a frying pan, add the onion and garlic and fry gently until lightly golden. Increase the heat slightly and pour in the wine. Let bubble until reduced by half, then stir in the chopped tomatoes, water and sugar. Season with salt and pepper. Simmer for 10–15 minutes until the tomatoes are soft, then remove the pan from the heat.

To cook the meatballs, heat the olive oil in a large, wide pan. Add the chilled meatballs and fry for 5 minutes, turning frequently, until browned all over. Pour the tomato sauce over them and simmer for a further 10–15 minutes until the meatballs are cooked through.

Divide the meatballs and tomato sauce between warm bowls and sprinkle with chopped parsley to serve.

Orange caramel
sauce

Put the demerara sugar into a dry, non-stick heavy-based pan and place over a high heat. Swirl the pan to ensure that the sugar melts evenly. Once all of the sugar has dissolved and formed a golden brown caramel, carefully pour in the orange juice – take care as the mixture will splutter. Don't worry if the hot caramel seizes upon contact with the cold juice. Over a gentle heat, swirl the pan frequently until the caramel has melted and the sauce is smooth. Take the pan off the heat.

Oranges in caramel
with sherry cream

THIS ELEGANT AND REFRESHING DESSERT is an ideal way to round off a rich meal. For a smart finishing touch, I've added some candied orange zest, but you can omit this for a more straightforward dessert. If you do prepare the candied orange zests and have some left over, save them to decorate other desserts or cakes.

SERVES 4

6 oranges
75g demerara sugar
100ml orange juice

Candied orange zest:
finely pared zest (in strips) from
   3 of the above oranges
250ml water
150g caster sugar

Sherry cream:
50ml double cream
2 tbsp icing sugar, sifted
1–2 tbsp medium sherry
few mint sprigs, to finish

To prepare the candied orange zest, remove any white pith from the zest strips, as this tastes very bitter, then slice the zest into thin strips. Pour the water into a small, heavy-based saucepan, add the caster sugar and dissolve over a medium heat, stirring frequently. Add the orange zest, partially cover and cook over a medium-low heat for 40–50 minutes until tender. Set aside to allow the zest to cool in the syrup.

To prepare the oranges, cut off the base and top from each one (including the 3 zested fruit) and cut away all the peel and pith, following the curve of the fruit. Turn each orange on its side and cut into 1cm slices. Overlap the slices on individual serving plates and chill.

Now prepare the orange caramel sauce, following my guide (on the preceding pages). Leave to cool completely.

For the sherry cream, in a large bowl, whip the cream with the icing sugar until it begins to thicken. Flavour with the sherry to taste and continue to whip until the cream holds soft peaks. Cover and chill until needed.

To serve, pour the cooled orange caramel sauce over the orange slices, then add a dollop of sherry cream. Scatter a little candied orange zest on top and finish with a sprig of mint. Serve at once.

Crema **Catalana**

SIMILAR TO THE FRENCH CRÈME BRÛLÉE but with a softer, thinner consistency, this delectable dessert holds an important place in Catalan cuisine. Traditionally, it is prepared by the matriarch of the family and served only on St. Joseph's Day, 19 March. Once tried, you may be tempted to make this creamy custard more than once a year.

SERVES 4–5

4 large egg yolks
70g caster sugar
2 tbsp cornflour, sifted
finely grated zest of 1 lemon
finely grated zest of 1 orange
1 cinnamon stick
250ml whole milk
250ml double cream
demerara sugar, to sprinkle

In a large bowl, whisk the egg yolks and caster sugar together until the mixture is pale and creamy. Whisk in the cornflour and lemon and orange zests, then add the cinnamon stick. Now slowly pour in the milk and cream, whisking continuously.

Transfer the mixture to a heavy-based saucepan and cook over a low heat, stirring constantly with a wooden spoon until the custard thickens enough to thickly coat the back of the spoon. At this stage, you should be able to feel some resistance as you stir the mixture. Do not overheat or it may curdle.

Remove from the heat and strain the custard through a fine sieve into a jug. Pour the custard into 4 or 5 ramekins, depending on size. Allow to cool completely, then transfer to the fridge and chill until needed.

Just before you are ready to serve, sprinkle a thin layer of demerara sugar over the surface of each custard. Caramelise the sugar by waving a cook's blowtorch over the surface. (If you don't have a blowtorch, place the ramekins on a baking sheet under a preheated very hot grill until the sugar is golden brown.) Either way, take care not to overheat the custards. Serve immediately.

BRITISH

SADLY, TRADITIONAL BRITISH FOOD HASN'T ENJOYED
A GREAT REPUTATION OVER THE YEARS, AS OTHER
'MORE EXCITING' CUISINES HAVE COME TO THE FORE.
RECENTLY, HOWEVER, SOME VERY TALENTED CHEFS
HAVE FOCUSED ON OUR FOOD HERITAGE AND HELPED
TO PUT BRITISH FOOD BACK ONTO MENUS. I'VE TRIED
TO HELP THE MOVEMENT BY SERVING ONLY BRITISH
FOOD IN MY PUBS AND THE FEEDBACK HAS BEEN
AMAZING. WE HAVE SOME OF THE BEST PRODUCE IN
THE WORLD – WE JUST NEED TO VALUE IT AND MAKE
THE MOST OF IT. HOPEFULLY, VISITORS TO THE UK
WILL APPRECIATE THAT THERE'S MUCH MORE TO OUR
FOOD CULTURE THAN FISH 'N' CHIPS!

Celery and **Stilton soup**
with Stilton toasts

IDEAL FOR USING UP STILTON after Christmas, this soup is a great winter warmer. It is substantial enough to serve as a lunch, with the Stilton toasts, and perhaps a chicory, walnut and clementine salad on the side.

SERVES 4

15g butter
1 tbsp olive oil
2 heads of celery, about 700g,
    trimmed and chopped
1 onion, peeled and chopped
sea salt and black pepper
800ml hot vegetable or chicken
    stock
100g Stilton, crumbled

Stilton toasts:
60g Stilton, crumbled
2 tbsp crème fraîche
handful of flat-leaf parsley,
    leaves chopped
2 slices of Granary or brown
    bread, crusts removed

Heat the butter and olive oil in a medium saucepan. Add the celery, onion and some seasoning and cook for 8–10 minutes, stirring frequently, until the vegetables are tender. Pour in just enough stock to cover and simmer for 3–5 minutes. Remove from the heat and let cool slightly.

Purée the soup using a free-standing blender, in batches if necessary, adding the Stilton as you go. Return the soup to the pan. Taste and adjust the seasoning if necessary.

For the Stilton toasts, preheat the grill to high. In a small bowl, mix the Stilton, crème fraîche and chopped parsley together and season lightly with salt and a good grinding of pepper. Lightly toast the bread on both sides. Spread with the Stilton mix and place under the grill until the cheese is melted and bubbling. Cut each slice in half diagonally.

Reheat the soup, ladle into warm serving bowls and grind over some pepper. Serve with the Stilton toasts on the side.

Warm Scottish **smoked salmon** and **watercress** salad

YOU CAN ASSEMBLE THIS LOVELY SALAD in minutes and enjoy it all year round. The hot-smoked salmon can be substituted with smoked trout or even peppery smoked mackerel if you like. When in season, use flavourful Jersey Royal potatoes for a real British treat.

SERVES 4–6

500g baby new potatoes, scrubbed
sea salt
300g hot smoked Scottish salmon
1/2 red onion, peeled and very thinly sliced
handful of dill, leaves roughly chopped
200g young, tender watercress

Dressing:
2 tbsp whisky
1 1/2 tbsp white wine vinegar
1 1/2 tbsp runny honey
1 1/2 tbsp grainy mustard
3 tbsp groundnut oil
3 tbsp olive oil
sea salt and black pepper

Add the new potatoes to a pan of salted water, bring to the boil and cook for 8–10 minutes until tender when pierced with a knife.

While the potatoes are cooking, prepare the dressing. Put the whisky, wine vinegar, honey, mustard, olive and groundnut oils in a small screw-topped jar, seal and shake vigorously to combine. Season with salt and pepper to taste and set aside.

Drain the potatoes and place in a large bowl. Flake the salmon into bite-sized pieces and add to the bowl along with the red onion and dill. Drizzle over some of the dressing and toss to coat.

Spread the potato and salmon mixture over a large platter, then scatter over the watercress. Drizzle with the remaining dressing and serve.

Baked egg and wild mushrooms

WILD MUSHROOMS TRANSFORM SIMPLE BAKED EGGS into a sophisticated starter. Serve with freshly made soda bread or hot buttered toast. This dish is also perfect as a brunch, if you serve two eggs per person and increase the quantities of the other ingredients slightly.

SERVES 4

20g butter, plus extra for greasing

400g wild mushrooms, cleaned and sliced

2 large shallots, peeled and finely chopped

few thyme sprigs, leaves picked

sea salt and black pepper

4 large eggs

4 tbsp double cream

25g mature Cheddar, grated

Place a frying pan over a high heat. Add the butter and when it begins to foam, toss the wild mushrooms, shallots and thyme leaves into the pan. Season with salt and pepper. Cook, stirring frequently, for 3–5 minutes.

Preheat the oven to 190°C/Fan 170°C/Gas 5. Lightly butter 4 individual gratin dishes and divide the mushroom mixture between them. Make a well in the centre and then carefully crack an egg into the well. Drizzle the cream around each egg and top with a sprinkling of grated cheese. Sprinkle with a pinch of salt and grind over some pepper.

Place the gratin dishes on a baking sheet and slide into the oven. Bake for 10–12 minutes for a runny yolk, or a couple of minutes longer if you prefer the yolk set. Serve at once, with soda bread or hot buttered toast.

Fish pie
with leeks and prawns

A GOLDEN POTATO-TOPPED FISH PIE is always a winner, especially during the colder months. I generally add a couple of egg yolks to the mash as they help to set the potato topping and give it a lovely shine.

SERVES 6

1 onion, peeled and quartered
3–4 cloves
1 bay leaf
250ml double cream
250ml whole milk
400g firm white fish fillets
400g smoked haddock fillets
30g butter
2 leeks, trimmed, well washed and thinly sliced
30g plain flour
sea salt and black pepper
handful of flat-leaf parsley, leaves chopped
300g peeled raw prawns

Topping:
750g Desirée potatoes, peeled
75g butter, cubed
50ml hot milk
2 large egg yolks
75–100g medium Cheddar, grated

Stud the onion with the cloves. Put into a wide pan along with the bay leaf, cream and milk and bring to a simmer. Lower the white and smoked fish fillets into the pan and poach for 3–4 minutes; it won't matter if the fish is slightly underdone at this stage. Lift it out of the pan onto a plate. Pass the cooking liquor through a fine sieve into a jug and reserve.

Melt the butter in a saucepan, add the leeks and sweat for 4–6 minutes until soft. Stir in the flour and cook, stirring, for another couple of minutes. Gradually stir in the reserved fish cooking liquor and let simmer for 10–15 minutes, stirring from time to time, until thickened to a sauce consistency. Season well with salt and pepper to taste and stir in the chopped parsley.

For the topping, cut the potatoes into chunks and add to a pan of salted water. Bring to the boil, lower the heat and cook for 15–20 minutes until tender when pierced with a knife. Drain well and push through a potato ricer, or mash until smooth. Add the butter and hot milk and mix until well incorporated. Allow to cool slightly, then stir in the egg yolks. Season well.

Preheat the oven to 200°C/Fan 180°C/Gas 6. Flake the fish into bite-sized pieces and add to the leek sauce with the prawns. Stir until evenly combined. Transfer to a 1.75–2 litre ovenproof baking dish and spoon the mash on top, spreading it evenly. For a traditional finish, mark the surface with the tines of a fork. Scatter over a generous layer of grated cheese. Bake in the oven for 25–30 minutes until the pie is bubbling and golden brown on top. Let stand for a few minutes, then serve with peas or green beans.

Rack of Welsh lamb with samphire

WELSH SALTMARSH LAMB AND SEA-SALTY SAMPHIRE are perfect partners for a summer roast. Samphire has a short season, peaking in July. It is available from fishmongers, as well as markets and selected supermarkets. When you can't get hold of any, serve the lamb racks with braised fennel or a simple watercress salad instead.

SERVES 4

2 racks of Welsh saltmarsh lamb, with 6 bones each
sea salt and black pepper
2 tbsp olive oil
200g samphire
25g butter
2–3 anchovy fillets, roughly chopped
grated zest and juice of 1/2 lemon
50g hazelnuts, halved and toasted

Preheat the oven to 200°C/Fan 180°C/Gas 6. Season the lamb racks with salt and pepper. Heat the olive oil in a large ovenproof pan or roasting tray and brown the lamb racks, fat-side down, for 2–3 minutes. Turn the racks fat side uppermost and transfer to the oven. Roast for 15 minutes for medium-rare meat, or 20 minutes for medium. Remove from the oven, cover loosely with foil and leave to rest in a warm place for at least 10 minutes.

Meanwhile, bring a large pan of salted water to the boil. Add the samphire and cook for 2–3 minutes until just tender. Refresh in a bowl of iced water, then drain again.

When you are almost ready to serve, melt the butter in a large frying pan over a medium-high heat. As it begins to foam, add the anchovy fillets, samphire, and lemon zest and juice. Warm through for 2–3 minutes, then add the toasted hazelnuts and a generous grinding of pepper.

To serve, divide the samphire between warm plates. Carve the lamb racks into individual chops and arrange on top of the samphire. Spoon over any pan juices from the samphire and lamb. Serve immediately, with new potatoes or a fluffy mash.

Pheasant casserole with winter vegetables and colcannon

THIS RUSTIC CASSEROLE TASTES EVEN BETTER the day after it has been made. Just be sure to reheat it gently so that the pheasant meat remains moist and succulent. Irish colcannon – creamy mash with shredded cabbage – makes a lovely accompaniment, but you could serve the casserole with ordinary mash and braised red cabbage if you prefer.

SERVES 6–8

2 pheasants, about 550g each
15g plain flour
sea salt and black pepper
3 tbsp olive oil
200g smoked bacon, cut into cubes
2 carrots, peeled and thickly sliced
2 large parsnips, peeled and cut into chunks
1/2 celeriac, peeled and cut into chunks
12 baby onions, peeled
2 tbsp runny honey
200ml red wine
few thyme sprigs
500ml chicken stock

Colcannon:
750g floury potatoes, such as Desirée or King Edward
1/2 Savoy cabbage, trimmed
80g butter, cut into cubes
75ml double cream, warmed

Preheat the oven to 180°C/Fan 160°C/Gas 4. Joint the pheasants. Season the flour with salt and pepper and use to lightly dust the pheasant pieces. Heat the olive oil in a large flameproof casserole and brown the pheasant pieces all over, in batches if necessary. Set aside on a plate.

Add the bacon cubes to the casserole and fry for 2–3 minutes, stirring frequently. Add the carrots, parsnips, celeriac and baby onions to the pan and fry, stirring, for 2–3 minutes until starting to soften. Add the honey, pour in the wine and cook until the liquid has reduced by half. Return the pheasants to the casserole, add the thyme and pour over the stock. Season with salt and pepper, put the lid on the casserole and place in the oven. Cook for 1–1 1/4 hours until the pheasant meat is tender.

Make the colcannon while the casserole is in the oven. Peel the potatoes and cut them into large, even-sized chunks. Add to a pan of salted water, bring to the boil and cook for 12–15 minutes until tender. Meanwhile, finely shred the cabbage. Place a frying pan over a medium heat and add a quarter of the butter. When it has melted, add the cabbage and sauté gently for 4–6 minutes until tender. Remove from the heat and set aside.

Drain the potatoes well, then return to the pan and place over a low heat to dry out for a minute. Take off the heat and pass through a potato ricer back into the pan, or mash well. Slowly stir in the cream, season well and gradually beat in the rest of the butter. Stir the cabbage through the mashed potato and check the seasoning.

Divide the pheasant casserole between warm plates and serve each portion with a generous helping of colcannon.

Gammon with pease pudding and parsley sauce

HEARTY, SIMPLE AND SATISFYING, boiled gammon and pease pudding makes a great weekday supper or casual Sunday lunch. A classic parsley sauce rounds off the dish perfectly. You'll just need to remember to put the gammon to soak the night before in plenty of cold water to remove excess salt.

SERVES 4

2kg boneless smoked gammon
   joint, soaked (see above)
1 onion, peeled and quartered
1 carrot, peeled and quartered
2 celery sticks, cut into chunks
2 bay leaves
few thyme sprigs
1 tsp black peppercorns

Pease pudding:
500g yellow split peas, soaked
   overnight in cold water
1 onion, peeled and quartered
1 carrot, peeled and quartered
2 bay leaves
2 tbsp malt vinegar
sea salt and white pepper
20g butter, cut into cubes

Parsley sauce:
20g butter
2 shallots, peeled and finely diced
20g plain flour
$1^{1}/_{2}$ tsp English mustard
150ml whole milk
handful of flat-leaf parsley,
   leaves chopped
1 tbsp double cream
lemon juice, to taste

Drain the gammon and place in a large saucepan with the onion, carrot, celery, bay leaves, thyme and black peppercorns. Pour on enough water to cover, then bring to the boil. Skim off any scum that rises to the surface. Lower the heat and simmer gently for about 2 hours, skimming occasionally, until the gammon is cooked through. Leave in the liquor.

For the pease pudding, drain the soaked peas and tip into a saucepan. Add the onion, carrot and bay leaves and cover with water (adding some of the stock from the gammon if it's not too salty). Bring to the boil and skim off any scum that rises to the surface. Lower the heat and simmer gently for an hour or until the peas are tender.

Discard the onion, carrot and bay leaves and tip the peas into a blender. Blitz to a purée, then pour into a clean pan. Add the vinegar and season with salt and pepper. Gradually beat in the butter, a cube at a time. Keep warm until ready to serve, adding a little water if it becomes too dry.

To make the parsley sauce, melt the butter in a small saucepan, add the shallots and sauté gently until softened but not coloured, 4–6 minutes. Add the flour and mustard, stir well and cook for a further 2–3 minutes. Gradually stir in the milk and 150ml strained liquor from the gammon. Bring to the boil, lower the heat and simmer for 6–8 minutes, stirring every so often. The sauce should be quite thick.

Just before serving, stir the chopped parsley, cream and a squeeze of lemon juice into the sauce and check the seasoning. Lift the gammon out of the liquor onto a board. Carve the meat into thick slices and warm through in some of the liquor if necessary. Serve with the pease pudding and parsley sauce.

5 ways with asparagus

Asparagus with lemon and tarragon hollandaise

For the hollandaise, cut 100g chilled unsalted butter into small cubes. Beat 2 large egg yolks with a squeeze of lemon juice, a cube of butter and some seasoning in a bowl set over a pan of simmering water until very thick and creamy. Beat in the rest of the butter, a cube at a time, then continue to beat until the hollandaise is shiny and thick. Season with sea salt, black pepper and lemon juice to taste and fold in some freshly chopped tarragon leaves. Blanch 450g trimmed asparagus in boiling salted water for 2–3 minutes until tender. Drain well and serve with the hollandaise. SERVES 4

Boiled egg and asparagus soldiers

Heat the oven to 200°C/Fan 180°C/Gas 6. Cut 8 prosciutto slices in half and wrap a half-slice around each of 16 asparagus spears. Lay on a lightly oiled baking sheet, drizzle with olive oil and grind over some black pepper. Bake for 10–12 minutes until the ham is crisp and the asparagus is tender. Meanwhile, add 4 large eggs to a pan of boiling salted water and boil for 4 minutes. Remove and place each one in an egg cup. Serve the boiled eggs at once, on warm plates with the asparagus soldiers. SERVES 4

Shaved asparagus and fennel salad

Finely slice 8–10 trimmed asparagus spears on the diagonal using a mandolin. Slice 1 trimmed medium fennel bulb in the same manner. Combine in a large bowl. Mix the juice of 1/2 lemon, 1/2 tsp Dijon mustard, 4 tbsp extra virgin olive oil, 1/2 tsp caster sugar and sea salt and black pepper to taste in a small bowl. Pour over the asparagus and fennel shavings and toss well. Cover and chill for at least 15–20 minutes. To serve, add about 100g tender watercress leaves, a handful of toasted pine nuts and some Parmesan shavings to the salad and toss lightly. SERVES 4

Asparagus, bacon and goat's cheese frittata

Heat 1 tbsp olive oil in a medium non-stick frying pan over a medium heat. Toss in 100g diced bacon and cook until lightly golden. Stir in 1 finely chopped garlic clove, 250g roughly chopped trimmed asparagus and some thyme leaves. Fry for 3–4 minutes until the asparagus is just tender. Meanwhile, beat 4 large eggs with 2–3 tbsp cream, 20g grated Parmesan and plenty of seasoning. Pour the egg mixture into the frying pan and stir gently to distribute the ingredients evenly. Scatter over 100g crumbled goat's cheese. Cook over a low heat, without stirring, until the eggs begin to set at the sides and on the bottom. Place the pan under a hot grill for 1–2 minutes until lightly set. Let stand for a minute before serving. SERVES 2

Asparagus and smoked salmon tartlets

Roll out 300g shortcrust pastry on a lightly floured surface to the thickness of a £1 coin and use to line 6 tartlet tins. Chill for at least 30 minutes. Blanch 200g trimmed asparagus in boiling salted water for 2–4 minutes until just tender. Drain, refresh in iced water, drain again and cut into 3cm lengths. Heat the oven to 200°C/Fan 180°C/Gas 6. Line the pastry cases with foil and baking beans and bake 'blind' for 15–20 minutes. Remove the foil and beans; bake for another 5 minutes. Lower the oven to 190°C/Fan 170°C/Gas 5. In a bowl, lightly beat 150ml double cream and 1 large egg with some sea salt and black pepper. Scatter 75g flaked hot-smoked salmon in the pastry cases and arrange the asparagus on top. Spoon over the cream mixture, then sprinkle with 20g grated Cheddar. Bake for 10–15 minutes until golden and set. Let cool slightly. SERVES 6

Steamed marmalade sponge pudding

A MOIST, STICKY STEAMED PUDDING IS DEEPLY COMFORTING and conjures up nostalgic childhood memories. Serve this one with a drizzle of pouring cream or custard, or – for an indulgent treat – clotted cream spiked with a little orange liqueur. If you have any to hand, top the pudding with candied orange zest (see page 102).

SERVES 4

140g butter, softened, plus extra for greasing
3 tbsp marmalade
2 tbsp golden syrup
finely grated zest of 1 orange
140g golden caster sugar
3 large eggs, lightly beaten
70g self-raising flour
2 tsp baking powder
2 tbsp whole milk

Lightly butter a 1.2 litre pudding basin. Mix 1 tbsp of the marmalade with the golden syrup and orange zest and spread over the bottom of the pudding basin.

Cream together the butter and sugar, using an electric mixer, until soft. With the motor still running, add the beaten eggs a little at a time, making sure each addition is fully incorporated before the next is added. Sift in the flour and baking powder and fold in alternately with the milk and remaining marmalade to obtain a smooth mixture. Spoon into the pudding basin.

Lay a pleated buttered sheet of greaseproof on top of the basin, buttered side down, and cover with a pleated sheet of foil, of the same size. Secure tightly with string under the rim of the basin.

Stand the basin on a trivet or upturned small heatproof plate in a large saucepan. Pour in enough boiling water to come halfway up the side of the basin and bring to a steady simmer. Cover with a tight-fitting lid and steam for $1\frac{1}{2}$ hours, checking the water level every 30 minutes or so, and topping up with boiling water as needed.

To check the pudding is ready, unwrap and insert a skewer into the sponge; it should come out clean. Unmould the hot pudding onto a warm serving plate and serve, with cream or custard.

Strawberry shortbread stacks

STRAWBERRIES AND CREAM epitomise the British summer. Fold them together and serve between shortbread rounds for a simple, yet elegant dessert. Home-made shortbread is unbeatable – you'll have more than you need for these stacks, but extras will keep well in an airtight tin for up to a week. If you are short of time, fine-quality bought shortbread will make this an almost instant dessert.

SERVES 4-6

Shortbread:

150g plain flour, plus extra to dust

100g rice flour

1/2 tsp fine sea salt

125g unsalted butter, at room
   temperature

90g caster sugar

1 large egg, beaten

Strawberry cream:

50ml double cream

150g clotted cream

3–4 tbsp icing sugar, sifted,
   plus extra to dust

1 vanilla pod, slit open lengthways

400g strawberries, hulled and
   quartered or cut into wedges

To make the shortbread, sift the flour, rice flour and salt together. Beat the butter and caster sugar together, using an electric mixer, until smooth. Add the egg slowly, then turn the machine to its lowest setting and add the flour, a spoonful at a time, until the mixture just comes together and forms a soft dough; do not overwork. Press the dough into a ball, wrap in cling film and chill for at least an hour.

Meanwhile, for the strawberry cream, put the double cream, clotted cream and icing sugar into a bowl and scrape in the seeds from the vanilla pod, using the tip of a knife. Beat until the mixture is thick and forms soft peaks. Set aside until you are ready to assemble the dessert.

Preheat the oven to 160°C/Fan 140°C/Gas 2½. On a lightly floured surface, roll out the dough to a 3–4mm thickness and cut out rounds, using a 9–10cm pastry cutter. Place the rounds on a baking sheet and bake in the oven for 20–25 minutes until pale golden. Leave on the baking sheet for a couple of minutes to firm up, then transfer to a wire rack and leave to cool completely.

To serve, fold the strawberries through the vanilla cream, reserving a handful. Put a shortbread in the centre of each plate and spoon the strawberry cream on top. Top with another shortbread round, lightly dust with icing sugar and place the reserved strawberries alongside.

Making custard

Put the milk, cream and 1 tbsp of the caster sugar into a heavy-based saucepan and slowly bring to the boil. Meanwhile, beat the egg yolks and the rest of the sugar together in a large bowl, using a hand whisk, until light and creamy. Just before the creamy milk comes to the boil, gradually pour it onto the egg and sugar mixture, whisking continuously. Strain the mixture through a fine sieve back into the pan and place over a low heat. Stir constantly with a wooden spoon until the custard thickens enough to coat the back of the spoon; do not overheat or it will curdle. Remove from the heat and strain the custard through a fine sieve once more.

Rhubarb fool

BEAUTIFUL BRIGHT PINK, FORCED RHUBARB makes
a delicious creamy fool. Lightly stew the fruit with vanilla and sugar,
allow to cool, then marry with a delicate custard. The rhubarb stems
break down easily when heated, so cook for less time if you prefer the
fruit to hold its shape and have a firmer texture.

SERVES 4–6

500g rhubarb
75g soft light brown sugar
finely grated zest and juice of
    1 orange
1 vanilla pod, slit open

Custard:
150ml whole milk
250ml double cream
50g caster sugar
6 large egg yolks

Cut the rhubarb stems into short lengths and place in a saucepan with
the brown sugar, orange zest and juice. Add a splash of water and scrape
the seeds from the vanilla pod into the pan, using the tip of a knife. Place
over a high heat. When the liquid begins to bubble, lower the heat and
simmer gently for 8–10 minutes or until the rhubarb is tender. Remove
from the heat and allow to cool completely, then chill.

Now make the custard, following my guide (on the preceding pages).
Pour into a chilled bowl and allow to cool, stirring every so often to
prevent a skin from forming. Chill until needed.

When ready to serve, lightly fold two-thirds of the chilled rhubarb
through the chilled custard. Drop a small spoonful of rhubarb into each
serving glass, then top with the rippled fool. Spoon the remaining
rhubarb on top and serve straight away.

MIDDLE EASTERN

FROM A CULINARY PERSPECTIVE, THE MIDDLE EAST
ENCOMPASSES COUNTRIES FROM AS FAR AS ALGERIA
AND MOROCCO IN THE WEST TO OMAN AND IRAN
IN THE EAST. THE VARIETY OF RESTAURANTS IN THE
UK HAVE GIVEN US A TASTE FOR AROMATIC NORTH
AFRICAN TAGINES AS WELL AS PERSIAN FOOD – RICH
WITH HERBS, SPICES AND FRUIT. AND IT'S NO LONGER
DIFFICULT TO SOURCE INGREDIENTS FOR A MIDDLE
EASTERN MEAL. I PARTICULARLY LOVE THE MEZE
CONCEPT OF SHARING A RANGE OF DISHES AT THE
START OF A MEAL – A CUSTOM THAT HELPS TO BRING
FAMILY AND FRIENDS TOGETHER THROUGH FOOD.

Courgette, feta and **herb** fritters

THESE TASTY VEGETARIAN FRITTERS are ideal as a light starter or as part of a meze spread. To prepare ahead, fry the fritters in advance and reheat them in a low oven when ready to serve.

SERVES 5–6

3 medium or 2 large courgettes, about 500g
sea salt and black pepper
2 tbsp light olive oil, plus extra to fry the fritters
1 large onion, peeled and thinly sliced
3 large eggs
200g feta, diced
small handful of mint sprigs, leaves chopped
small handful of dill sprigs, leaves chopped
2 tbsp pine nuts
3–4 tbsp plain flour

To serve:
lemon wedges
flat-leaf parsley sprigs (optional)

Trim the courgettes and coarsely grate them into a sieve set on top of a bowl. Sprinkle over a pinch of salt, mix well and leave to stand for about 10 minutes. (The salt will help to draw out excess moisture.) Squeeze the grated courgettes with your hands to remove some of the juices, then tip into a large bowl.

Meanwhile, heat 2 tbsp olive oil in a wide frying pan and sauté the onion, with a pinch each of salt and pepper, for 5–6 minutes until softened. Leave to cool slightly, then add to the courgettes and mix well.

Add the eggs, feta, chopped herbs, pine nuts and 3 tbsp flour to the courgette mixture. Add a generous grinding of pepper and mix well until evenly combined. (As the feta is salty, you probably won't need to add salt.) If the batter seems too wet, add another 1 tbsp flour and mix well.

Heat a thin layer of olive oil in a wide frying pan. You will need to fry the fritters in batches: drop several spoonfuls of the batter into the pan, spacing them apart, and fry for 2–3 minutes on each side until golden brown. Transfer to a warm plate lined with kitchen paper and keep warm while you cook the rest; there should be enough for 20–24 small fritters.

Serve the courgette fritters warm, with lemon wedges and a parsley garnish, if you like.

Spinach and feta filo rolls

IN MOROCCO, THESE ARE MADE with thin warka pastry and a plain cheese filling, but I've used filo here, as it's more accessible, and added spinach to the filling to give it another dimension. Serve as a starter or meze dish.

SERVES 4-6

1 tbsp olive oil
150g spinach leaves, washed and drained
200g feta
1 large egg, beaten
small bunch of mixed herbs, such as mint, flat-leaf parsley and dill, leaves chopped
sea salt and black pepper
pinch of sumac (optional)
6 sheets of filo pastry
100g unsalted butter, melted

Heat a frying pan and add the olive oil. When hot, add the spinach and stir until wilted. Tip into a colander and press with the back of a ladle to squeeze out excess moisture, then pat dry with kitchen paper. Chop the spinach finely and place in a large bowl. Leave to cool.

Preheat the oven to 200°C/Fan 180°C/Gas 6. Crumble the feta over the spinach and mix in the egg, chopped herbs, seasoning and a pinch of sumac, if using.

Work with 2 filo pastry sheets at a time, keeping the rest covered with a tea towel to prevent them from drying out. Brush a sheet of filo pastry with melted butter, then press the second sheet on top. Brush again with melted butter, then cut through both layers into 4 even rectangles.

Spread a tablespoonful of the feta and spinach filling along one short end of a filo rectangle, leaving a 2cm margin on both sides. Roll the pastry over the filling just to enclose it, then tuck in the ends on both sides and continue to roll up the 'cigar' to the end. Place on a large lightly buttered baking sheet and brush with more melted butter. Repeat with the rest of the filo to use up all the filling; you should have enough for 12 rolls.

Bake the filo rolls in the oven for 20–30 minutes until golden and crisp. Best served warm from the oven.

Falafel with tahini sauce

FALAFEL ARE RELATIVELY EASY TO MAKE and far tastier than the ubiquitous ready-made versions in supermarkets and sandwich shops. For an authentic, nutty flavour and texture, you do need to use soak dried chickpeas overnight, but there is no need to boil them before you make the falafel.

SERVES 4–5

Falafel:

300g dried chickpeas, soaked in plenty of water overnight
sea salt and black pepper
2 tsp dried mint
2 tsp ground cumin
2 tsp ground coriander
1 tsp bicarbonate of soda
finely grated zest of 1 lemon
2 garlic cloves, peeled and finely chopped
1/2 medium onion, peeled and finely chopped
small bunch of coriander, leaves chopped
vegetable or groundnut oil, for shallow-frying

Tahini sauce:

1 tbsp tahini (sesame seed paste)
3 tbsp Greek yoghurt
1–2 tbsp lemon juice, to taste
1 tsp runny honey
1–2 tbsp warm water (optional)

Drain and rinse the chickpeas, then drain thoroughly. Tip them into a food processor and whiz with a pinch of salt to the consistency of coarse breadcrumbs. Add the rest of the ingredients, except the oil, and blend until the mixture is well combined with a fine crumb texture.

Tip the mixture into a large bowl and check for seasoning. Now shape it into balls, each about the size of a golf ball. Place on a tray, cover with cling film and chill for 30 minutes to firm up.

For the tahini sauce, mix all the ingredients together in a bowl until smooth and season with salt and pepper to taste. For a thinner consistency, if required, loosen with 1–2 tbsp warm water.

To cook the falafel, heat a 2cm depth of oil in a frying pan. You will need to shallow-fry them in batches. Carefully lower several into the hot oil, one at a time. Fry for 4–5 minutes, turning them occasionally, until golden and crisp. Drain each batch on kitchen paper and keep warm in a low oven while you cook the rest.

Serve the falafels with the tahini sauce. Accompany with warm pitta breads and a mixed salad drizzled with a little of the tahini sauce if liked.

Shaping dolmades

Lay a vine leaf, shiny-side down, on a clean surface. Place a heaped teaspoonful of the filling in the middle of the leaf, nearer to the stem edge. Fold over the stem end to cover the filling, then tuck in both sides of the vine leaf and roll up like a cigar. Repeat with the remaining vine leaves and filling.

Dolmades

THESE STUFFED VINE LEAVES ARE NOT DIFFICULT to make, but rolling them does take time, particularly as I usually double the recipe to feed a crowd. I try to make it a family affair and enlist the kids' help – the best way to persuade them that something is really good to eat. If you are cooking the rice from scratch, you'll need about 200g uncooked weight.

SERVES 4

230g packet vine leaves in brine
2 tbsp olive oil, plus extra to
    drizzle
1 large onion, peeled and finely
    chopped
2 garlic cloves, peeled and finely
    chopped
400g cooked white rice, preferably
    long-grain
100g pine nuts, toasted
100g sultanas
1/4 tsp ground allspice
1/2 tsp ground cinnamon
pinch of caster sugar
2 ripe tomatoes, skinned,
    deseeded and chopped
small handful of flat-leaf parsley,
    chopped
small handful of mint, chopped
sea salt and black pepper
about 300ml vegetable stock
juice of 1/2 lemon, plus extra
    to drizzle
extra virgin olive oil, to drizzle

Baba ganoush (top); dolmades (left); tabbouleh (right)

To remove excess salt from the vine leaves, put them into a large bowl and pour on boiling water to cover. Leave to soak for a few minutes, then carefully drain off the liquid. Rinse under cold water and drain again.

Heat the olive oil in a pan and gently fry the onion and garlic for a few minutes, stirring occasionally, until softened. Tip into a bowl and add the cooked rice, pine nuts, sultanas, allspice, cinnamon, sugar, tomatoes, herbs and seasoning. Taste and adjust the seasoning (as the dolmades will be served cold, you need to season generously).

Now stuff the vine leaves with the rice filling, following my guide (on the preceding pages).

Drape a clean, wet tea towel in a wide pan to lie flat on the base, with the sides overhanging the edge of the pan. Pack the vine leaves on top in tight, neat layers. Add the stock, lemon juice and a drizzle of olive oil.

Cover the dolmades with a piece of baking parchment, and then place a small heatproof plate that just fits inside the pan on top. (This will prevent the dolmades from unwrapping during cooking.) Cover the pan with a lid and simmer gently for an hour.

Remove the plate and then carefully take the dolmades out of the pan by lifting the tea towel. Transfer to a tray and leave to cool. Chill for a few hours, or overnight if preparing ahead. Take the dolmades out of the fridge 10 minutes before serving. Drizzle with a little extra virgin olive oil and lemon juice to serve.

Baba ganoush

FROM THE LEVANT THROUGH TO TURKEY AND EGYPT,
this lovely aubergine dip is popular throughout the Middle East.
Naturally, there are slight variations on the seasoning and ingredients
used, depending on where you are. The aubergines can either be
roasted or grilled over an open flame until the flesh is soft and smoky.
Prepare the dip in advance and serve at room temperature.

SERVES 4–6

2 large aubergines, about
   600–650g
a little oil, for oiling
juice of $1/2$ lemon, or to taste
$1^1/_2$ tbsp tahini (sesame seed
   paste)
2 tbsp natural yoghurt
2 fat garlic cloves, peeled and
   crushed
1 thyme sprig, leaves picked
sea salt and black pepper

To serve:
extra virgin olive oil, to drizzle
few pinches of sumac, or a little
   chopped flat-leaf parsley,
   to sprinkle

Preheat the oven to 220°C/Fan 200°C/Gas 7. Prick each aubergine
several times with the tip of a sharp knife, then place both on a lightly
oiled baking sheet. Roast in the hot oven for 45–60 minutes, turning them
over halfway, until the skins are wrinkly and the aubergines feel soft
when lightly pressed; they should almost collapse upon themselves.

Leave the aubergines until cool enough to handle, then peel away the
blackened skins and put the flesh into a colander. Press with the back of
a ladle to squeeze out as much liquid as possible, then tip the aubergine
flesh onto a board and chop roughly (or blitz in a blender for a smooth
texture if preferred).

Put the chopped aubergine into a bowl and add the lemon juice, tahini,
yoghurt, garlic, thyme leaves and seasoning. Mix well, then taste and
adjust the seasoning. (Cover and chill if not serving immediately.)

Spoon the baba ganoush into a serving bowl and drizzle a little extra
virgin olive oil over the surface. Sprinkle with a little sumac or chopped
parsley to garnish and serve, with warm flat breads.

Illustrated on page 142

Tabbouleh

A GORGEOUS BULGUR WHEAT SALAD teeming with freshly chopped herbs, tomatoes and spring onions. Traditional tabbouleh recipes use fine ground bulgur wheat, which is available at delis and Middle Eastern grocers if you would prefer to use it. This salad is best mixed when you are about to serve it, as the lemon juice will discolour the herbs with time. Serve the dish as a meze or accompaniment to fish and meat dishes.

SERVES 4–6

75g bulgur wheat
250g ripe plum tomatoes
juice of 1 small lemon, or to taste
3 tbsp extra virgin olive oil
sea salt and black pepper
3 spring onions, trimmed
bunch of flat-leaf parsley, about 75g
bunch of mint, about 75g
seeds from ½ small pomegranate, to garnish
   (optional)

Put the bulgur wheat into a bowl, pour on boiling water to cover generously, then cover the bowl with cling film and leave the grains to swell for 10 minutes. Tip the bulgur wheat into a fine sieve and drain very thoroughly, then return to the bowl.

Finely dice the tomatoes and add to the bulgur wheat, along with the lemon juice, extra virgin olive oil and some salt and pepper. Mix well, using a fork, and then leave the bulgur to soak up the juices and soften a little more. Taste and adjust the seasoning.

Meanwhile, finely chop the spring onions and roughly shred the parsley and mint leaves with a sharp knife. When you are ready to serve, fold the herbs through the bulgur wheat and garnish with a scattering of pomegranate seeds, if you wish.

Illustrated on page 142

Pan-fried **red mullet** with **saffron pilaf** and **tarator** sauce

IN LEBANON AND TURKEY, LOCAL FISH are often fried and served with tarator sauce and saffron rice. Here I'm serving red mullet fillets, but any firm white fish can be prepared in the same way. Save any leftover sauce to serve with grilled meat or poultry.

SERVES 4

4 red mullet, about 400g each,
   filleted (skin on)
2 tbsp plain flour
1/2 tsp ground cumin
1/2 tsp ground ginger
1/2 tsp ground cinnamon
sea salt and black pepper
2–3 tbsp olive oil

Saffron rice pilaf:
4 tbsp olive oil
2 large onions, peeled and finely
   sliced
300g long-grain rice
600ml hot chicken or vegetable
   stock
pinch of saffron strands
75g pine nuts, toasted
handful of flat-leaf parsley, leaves
   chopped

Tarator sauce:
4 tbsp tahini (sesame seed paste)
50g pine nuts, toasted
3 tbsp lemon juice, or to taste
1 garlic clove, peeled and chopped
1/2 tsp ground cumin
pinch of cayenne pepper
3–4 tbsp hot water

Check the fish for small bones, removing any with kitchen tweezers. Set aside at room temperature while you prepare the pilaf.

For the saffron rice pilaf, heat half the olive oil in a medium heavy-based saucepan. Add the onions with a pinch each of salt and pepper and sauté for 5–6 minutes until starting to soften. Add the remaining oil and tip in the rice. Stir well and cook, stirring, for a minute, then add the stock and saffron. Bring to a simmer, cover with a tight-fitting lid and cook for 8–10 minutes, just until most of the stock has been absorbed. Turn off the heat and leave the rice to steam in the covered pan for another 5 minutes.

While the rice is cooking, make the tarator sauce. Put the tahini, pine nuts, lemon juice, garlic, cumin, cayenne and some seasoning into a food processor and blitz on high speed. With the machine running, add the water, 1 tbsp at a time, until the sauce is smooth with the consistency of a light mayonnaise. Adjust the flavour to taste, with additional lemon juice or salt. Transfer to a serving bowl.

About 5 minutes before the rice will be ready, cook the fish. Season the flour with the cumin, ginger, cinnamon and some salt and pepper and use to coat the red mullet fillets. Heat the olive oil in a wide frying pan until hot. Fry the fillets for 1 1/2–2 minutes on each side until golden brown and just cooked through; the fish should feel just firm when lightly pressed.

Serve the fish on the saffron rice with a generous spoonful of tarator sauce alongside. Scatter over the pine nuts and chopped parsley. Put the remaining sauce in a bowl on the table for guests to help themselves.

Lamb tagine with apricots and herb couscous

LAMB AND FRUIT GO WELL TOGETHER and this stew includes some tangy preserved lemons to balance out the sweetness of the dried fruit. When fresh apricots are in season, you can use 200g of these instead: cut into wedges, discarding the stones, and add to the stew once the lamb is tender – they'll only need a few minutes to soften; you may need to add a little more honey, too.

SERVES 4

900g boned lamb shoulder
2 tbsp plain flour
sea salt and black pepper
4 tbsp olive oil
1 large onion, peeled and finely sliced
2 garlic cloves, peeled and crushed
1 tbsp grated fresh root ginger
1½ tbsp ras el hanout (Moroccan spice mix)
1½ tbsp tomato purée
about 800ml lamb or chicken stock
100g dried apricots, chopped
1½ preserved lemons, chopped
squeeze of lemon juice
2 tbsp runny honey, or to taste

Herb couscous:
500ml chicken or vegetable stock
300g couscous
large handful of flat-leaf parsley
large handful of mint
small handful of coriander
finely grated zest of 1 lemon
2 tsp lemon juice
2 tbsp extra virgin olive oil

Cut the lamb into bite-sized chunks. Season the flour with salt and pepper and toss the lamb in it to coat. Heat half the olive oil in a large heavy-based pan or flameproof casserole and brown the meat in batches, turning to colour all over and transferring to a plate once browned.

Add the onion and a little more oil to the pan, if necessary, and sauté for 5 minutes until it starts to soften. Add the garlic, ginger, ras el hanout and tomato purée and fry for a few minutes until fragrant. Return the lamb and any juices to the pan and stir well.

Pour in enough stock to cover everything and bring to the boil, then reduce to a simmer. Skim the surface frequently until the stock is clear, then partially cover the pan with the lid and cook gently, stirring occasionally, for 1½ hours.

Stir in the apricots, preserved lemons, lemon juice and honey to taste. Simmer, uncovered, for a further 30–45 minutes, stirring frequently, until the lamb is tender. Taste and adjust the seasoning. (The stew can be prepared ahead and reheated before serving, if more convenient.)

To make the couscous, bring the stock to the boil. Tip the couscous into a large bowl, then pour on the stock. Cover the bowl tightly with cling film and leave for 10–15 minutes until all the stock has been absorbed. Meanwhile, strip the herb leaves from their stalks and chop them.

Fluff up the couscous with a fork to separate the grains, then fork through the herbs, lemon zest and some seasoning. Mix the lemon juice and extra virgin olive oil together, then fork through the couscous and check the seasoning. Serve with the lamb tagine.

Turkish yoghurt cake with citrus syrup

THIS MOIST, DENSE YOGHURT CAKE has a similar texture to a light cheesecake. The citrus syrup gives the top a lovely sheen and imparts a tangy sweetness. Save any leftover syrup to drizzle over cold vanilla ice cream, plain yoghurt or breakfast pancakes.

SERVES 8

butter, for greasing
6 large eggs, separated
150g caster sugar
75g self-raising flour
600g strained natural Greek
    yoghurt
finely grated zest and juice of
    1 lemon
pinch of fine sea salt

Citrus syrup:
125g caster sugar
125ml water
finely pared zest and juice of
    1 lemon
finely pared zest and juice of
    1 orange
1 tsp orange blossom water
    (or rosewater)

Preheat the oven to 180°C/Fan 160°C/Gas 4. Butter the base and sides of a 23–25cm round cake tin with removable base and line the base with a disc of baking parchment.

Beat the egg yolks and sugar together with a hand-held electric whisk until pale and creamy. Sift the flour over the surface and fold in gently. Add the yoghurt, lemon zest and juice, and fold through.

In another large, clean bowl, whisk the egg whites with a pinch of salt until firm peaks form. Carefully fold them into the cake mixture, using a large metal spoon.

Pour the mixture into the prepared cake tin and gently level the surface. Bake in the oven for 50–60 minutes until the cake is golden brown on top, risen and cooked through. To test, insert a skewer inserted into the middle; it should come out clean. Leave to cool completely in the tin; the cake will sink slightly as it cools.

While the cake is in the oven, prepare the citrus syrup. Put all of the ingredients into a saucepan and bring to the boil. Lower the heat slightly and simmer for about 7–10 minutes until it has reduced by a third and is syrupy. Leave to cool, then pour into a serving jug.

Turn the cake out onto a large plate or cake stand and spoon some citrus syrup evenly all over the surface. Serve with some crème fraîche or thick yoghurt on the side, if you like.

Almond semolina cake

THIS DELICIOUS LEBANESE CAKE is known as *sfouf* and acquires its lovely yellow colour from the inclusion of a little turmeric. This is a fairly large cake, but one that keeps well in an airtight container in the fridge for up to 5 days. Serve with hot mint tea or Turkish coffee at the end of a meal, or at teatime.

SERVES 10–12

butter, for greasing
450g fine semolina
150g plain flour
1 tsp ground turmeric
2 tsp baking powder
450g caster sugar
550ml whole milk
2 large eggs, lightly beaten
200g lightly salted butter, melted
1 tsp orange blossom water (or rosewater)
25g flaked almonds
2 tbsp apricot jam, warmed, to glaze (optional)

To serve (optional):
thick yoghurt
runny honey, to drizzle

Preheat the oven to 180°C/Fan 160°C/Gas 4. Lightly butter a 23cm square cake tin (or a 24cm round tin), preferably with a removable base, and line the base with baking parchment.

In a large bowl, combine the semolina, flour, turmeric and baking powder. Stir to mix, then make a well in the centre.

In a separate bowl, mix the sugar, milk, eggs, melted butter and orange blossom water together until evenly blended. Pour into the well in the dry ingredients and fold together until well combined. Pour the mixture into the prepared cake tin and sprinkle the almonds over the surface.

Bake for 40–50 minutes until the top is golden brown and the cake is cooked though. To test, insert a skewer into the centre; it should come out clean. Leave in the tin for about 15–20 minutes before unmoulding onto a wire rack to cool. If you wish, brush the top of the cake with a little apricot jam to glaze.

Slice the cake and serve – either on its own or with a dollop of yoghurt drizzled with a little honey.

CHINESE

A MEAL AT OUR FAVOURITE LOCAL CHINESE IS ALWAYS
A TREAT – THE KIDS LOVE IT AND I ENCOURAGE THEM
TO TRY SOMETHING DIFFERENT EACH TIME. NOT
SURPRISINGLY, AS CHINA IS SUCH A VAST COUNTRY,
THE COOKING VARIES SIGNIFICANTLY FROM ONE REGION
TO ANOTHER. GINGER, GARLIC AND SPRING ONIONS
ARE COMMON INGREDIENTS. TOGETHER WITH VARIOUS
SOY SAUCES, THEY ARE USED TO CREATE ALL MANNER
OF TASTY DISHES. IF YOU ONLY COOK ONE RECIPE FROM
THIS CHAPTER, MAKE IT THE PORK BELLY – IT MELTS
IN THE MOUTH AND THE FLAVOUR IS SUBLIME.

Sweetcorn and crab soup

ORIGINALLY CREATED BY CHINESE EMIGRANTS in America, this easy soup now appears on Chinese restaurant menus in most countries. Creamed sweetcorn provides the right texture for the soup, but if you are having difficulty finding it, buy tinned sweetcorn kernels and pulse them in a food processor to a rough purée.

SERVES 4–6

125g white crabmeat
2 large egg whites
1 tbsp cornflour, mixed with 2 tbsp water
1.2 litres chicken stock
2.5cm knob of fresh root ginger, peeled and grated
225g tin creamed sweetcorn
sea salt and white pepper
2 spring onions, trimmed and finely sliced

Pick through the crabmeat with your fingers and remove any stray fragments of shell. In another bowl, lightly beat the egg whites until frothy. Add them to the crabmeat along with the blended cornflour and stir well.

Pour the stock into a saucepan, add the ginger and bring to a simmer. Tip in the sweetcorn and bring back to the boil. Lower the heat slightly and simmer for a few minutes. Stir in the crabmeat mixture and some seasoning. Simmer gently, stirring, for a few minutes until the soup has thickened. Taste and adjust the seasoning.

Ladle the soup into warm bowls and scatter the spring onion slices on top. Serve immediately.

Crispy salt and pepper squid
with cucumber salad

DEEP-FRIED SQUID IS A MUCH-LOVED DISH and almost every cuisine seems to have a different version. Here Szechuan pepper and five-spice powder give the squid an extra kick. When deep-frying, keep the oil at a constant high temperature to ensure the squid cooks and crispens quickly. Avoid overcooking, otherwise the squid will turn tough and rubbery.

SERVES 4

400g baby squid, cleaned
1/2 tsp Szechuan peppercorns
1 tsp sea salt
1 tsp freshly ground black pepper
1/4 tsp five-spice powder
5 heaped tbsp cornflour
vegetable or groundnut oil, for
    deep-frying

Cucumber salad:
1 medium cucumber
1 medium carrot
1 red chilli, deseeded and finely
    sliced
handful of coriander leaves
3 tbsp rice vinegar
1/2 tsp sea salt
1 tsp caster sugar
1 tsp sesame oil

To serve:
1 red chilli, trimmed and finely
    sliced, to garnish
small handful of coriander leaves,
    to garnish
lime wedges

First, prepare the cucumber salad. Peel the cucumber and carrot, then slice into long strips, using a vegetable peeler or a mandolin. Cut the strips in half if they are too long. Toss them in a bowl with the red chilli and coriander leaves. In a small bowl, mix together the rice vinegar, salt, sugar and sesame oil; set aside.

Slice the squid pouches into thick rings, leaving the tentacles whole. Rinse and pat dry with kitchen paper. Using a pestle and mortar, grind the Szechuan peppercorns with the salt to a fine powder. Tip into a small bowl and mix in the black pepper, five-spice powder and cornflour.

Heat a 5cm depth of oil in a wok over a high heat until a piece of bread dropped into the hot oil sizzles vigorously. Deep-fry the squid rings and tentacles in batches: coat with the seasoned cornflour, shake off excess, then immerse in the hot oil, taking care not to overcrowd the wok. Deep-fry for about a minute until lightly golden and crisp, then remove with a slotted spoon and drain on kitchen paper. Keep warm in a low oven while you deep-fry the rest of the squid.

Toss the cucumber salad with the dressing and divide between serving plates. Pile the crispy squid on top and scatter over the sliced chilli and coriander leaves. Serve with lime wedges.

Shaping Chinese dumplings

On a lightly floured surface, roll out the pastry dough into a long sausage, about 2.5cm thick. Cut into 2cm lengths. Flatten each piece with the palm of your hand, then roll out into a thin round, approximately 9cm in diameter.

Put 1–1$\frac{1}{2}$ teaspoonfuls of filling in the centre of a round and brush the rim of the pastry with a little water. Fold the sides up over the filling to meet, creating a half-moon shape. Now carefully pinch the edges of the pastry together using your fingertips, making small folds, or pleats, along one side. Set aside. Repeat to make the rest of the dumplings.

Pork and prawn dumplings

MAKING CHINESE DUMPLINGS is a labour of love, requiring patience, time and practice. If you are going to the effort, it is worth making a large batch so that you can freeze some for another meal. Freeze, uncooked, on a tray lined with parchment, then pack into a rigid container. Defrost at room temperature before cooking.

MAKES 30–35

Pastry:
300g plain flour, plus extra to dust
1 tsp fine sea salt
1 tbsp vegetable oil
120–150ml cold water

Filling:
200g Chinese cabbage leaves
sea salt and white pepper
250g minced pork
200g raw prawns, peeled, deveined and finely chopped
3cm knob of fresh root ginger, peeled and grated
1 tsp soft light brown sugar
2 tbsp light soy sauce
1 tbsp Chinese rice wine (or dry sherry)
2 tsp sesame oil

Dipping sauce:
2 tbsp red chilli oil (available from Asian grocers)
1 tbsp light soy sauce
1 large garlic clove, peeled and finely chopped
1 spring onion, trimmed, green part only, finely sliced

To make the pastry for the dumplings, mix the flour and salt together in a large bowl and make a well in the centre. Add the oil and 120ml water. Mix with a round-bladed knife until the mixture starts to come together as a firm dough. Add a little more water if it seems too dry. Knead the dough on a lightly floured surface for 5–10 minutes until silky. Shape into a ball, wrap in cling film and leave to rest while you make the filling.

For the filling, add the cabbage leaves to a pan of boiling salted water and blanch for 2–3 minutes until just wilted. Drain well and pat dry with kitchen paper. Chop the leaves finely and place in a large bowl. Add the rest of the filling ingredients and mix well. To check the seasoning, fry off a little ball of the mixture in an oiled pan, then taste for seasoning. Adjust the seasoning of the uncooked filling mixture as necessary.

Now roll out the pastry dough and shape the dumplings, following my guide (on the preceding pages).

You will need to cook the dumplings in batches. Steam them in a bamboo steamer lined with baking parchment for 7–10 minutes until just cooked through (or you can poach them in a light stock for 5 minutes if you prefer, then drain well).

While the dumplings are cooking, mix all the ingredients for the dipping sauce together and divide between individual dipping bowls. Serve the dumplings, freshly cooked and piping hot, with the dipping sauce.

Steamed bream with ginger and spring onions

STEAMING WHOLE FISH IN THIS WAY enables you to retain all of its wonderful, flavourful juices and gives you a lovely, aromatic sauce – perfect for spooning over accompanying plain white rice.

SERVES 4

1 bream, scaled and gutted, about 700g
4cm knob of fresh root ginger, peeled
4 spring onions, trimmed
1 long red chilli, deseeded
2 tbsp Shaoxing or Chinese rice wine (or dry sherry)
2 tbsp light soy sauce
2 tbsp sesame oil

Make slashes in the fish, about 2.5cm apart, slightly on the diagonal, without cutting right through to the bone. Slice the ginger, spring onions and red chilli lengthways into thin matchsticks.

Scatter a little ginger and spring onion over a heatproof plate, large enough to take the fish. Lay the bream on the plate and stuff the fish cavity with a little ginger, spring onion and chilli. Drizzle the rice wine and soy sauce over the fish, then scatter over the rest of the ginger, spring onion and chilli.

Place an inverted heatproof bowl in a large wok and pour in enough water to come halfway up the sides of the bowl. Put the lid on the wok and bring the water to the boil. Now carefully lower the plate containing the fish into the pan, placing it on the upturned bowl; avoid touching the sides of the hot wok. Put the lid back on and steam over a high heat until the fish is just cooked – a knife should slide easily into the thickest part of the flesh. It will take about 10–15 minutes.

As soon as the fish is ready, carefully lift the plate from the steamer. Heat the sesame oil in a small pan until smoking hot, then immediately pour over the fish. Bring the plate to the table and serve at once, with rice and a vegetable dish on the side.

Red braised pork belly

REPUTED TO BE MAO ZEDONG'S FAVOURITE dish, this is a speciality of Hunan, his home region. It is irresistibly rich and truly delicious. Enjoy with a simple bowl of steamed white rice and pak choi or a mixed vegetable stir-fry.

SERVES 4–6

800g pork belly
1 tbsp vegetable oil
2 tbsp rock sugar
  (or caster sugar)
3 tbsp light soy sauce
3 tbsp dark soy sauce
3cm knob of fresh root ginger,
  peeled and thickly sliced
2 star anise
1 cinnamon stick
3 dried red chillies
about 200ml water
3 spring onions, trimmed and
  chopped

Bring a wide pan of water to the boil, then reduce the heat slightly. Lower the pork belly into the pan (cut in half if it doesn't fit in whole) and simmer for 3–4 minutes. Skim off the scum and froth from the surface; there will be a lot of it. Drain the pork belly and leave to cool slightly. Rinse out the pan and return to the hob.

Cut the pork belly into 2cm cubes. Heat the oil and sugar in the pan over a medium heat. Once the sugar is melted and beginning to caramelise, add the pork pieces, skin-side down, and fry for a few minutes until the skin begins to caramelise.

Add the soy sauces, ginger, star anise, cinnamon and dried chillies to the pan and pour in enough water to just cover the meat. Bring to a gentle simmer and cook for about 50–60 minutes until the pork is very tender.

Remove the pork with a slotted spoon and set aside on a plate. Boil the sauce until reduced and syrupy, then taste and adjust the seasoning, adding a little more sugar if you find it too salty. Stir in the spring onions, reserving a handful for serving, and return the pork pieces to the pan to warm through.

Pile the pork into a warm bowl, sprinkle with the remaining spring onions and serve at once.

Five-spice roast duck with plum sauce

THIS TENDER AROMATIC DUCK is perfectly complemented by my spiced fresh plum sauce. Serve it topped with shredded spring onions and cucumber, and if you wish, accompany with thin, ready-made Chinese pancakes. Any leftovers will be lovely with noodles.

SERVES 6–8

1 duckling, about 2.25kg
1 tsp sea salt
1 tsp five-spice powder
1 tsp black pepper
1 tbsp soy sauce
2 tbsp runny honey
2 tbsp Chinese black vinegar
   (or lemon juice)

Fresh plum sauce:
1 tbsp vegetable oil
1 tsp grated fresh root ginger
3 ripe plums, stoned and chopped
1/2 tsp five-spice powder
1 small cinnamon stick
2 star anise
2 tbsp Chinese rice vinegar
4 tbsp soft brown sugar
1–2 tbsp water

To serve:
thinly shredded spring onions
thinly sliced cucumber

Preheat the oven to 220°C/Fan 200°C/Gas 7. Remove as much fat as possible from around the neck of the duck. In a small bowl, mix together the salt, five-spice powder and pepper. Lightly score the skin of the duck, then rub the seasoning mixture all over the skin and into the cuts.

Place the duck, breast-side up, on a wire rack set on top of a roasting tray. Place in the hot oven and roast for 30 minutes.

In the meantime, mix the soy sauce, honey and Chinese vinegar together in a small bowl. Carefully baste the duck with the soy mixture and pour a cupful of water into the roasting tray. Lower the oven setting to 190°C/Fan 170°C/Gas 5 and roast the duck for a further 1¼–1½ hours, basting every half-hour or so, until it is tender and just cooked through.

While the duck is roasting, make the plum sauce. Heat a little oil in a pan, add the ginger and cook until lightly golden, about 1–2 minutes. Tip in the chopped plums, five-spice powder, cinnamon, star anise, rice vinegar and sugar. Stir well and simmer for about 15 minutes until the mixture has a thick, jammy consistency. Transfer to a serving bowl. The sauce can be served warm or at room temperature.

Once the duck is cooked, cover loosely with foil and leave to rest in a warm place for 15–20 minutes. Carve and arrange on a large platter. Scatter over some shredded spring onions and sliced cucumber and serve, with the plum sauce.

5 ways with Chinese greens

Chinese **broccoli** with **oyster sauce**

Trim 450g Chinese broccoli (kai lan), wash and drain well, then cut into finger lengths. In a bowl, mix 1 tbsp Chinese rice wine (or dry sherry), $\frac{1}{4}$ tsp caster sugar, 3 tbsp oyster sauce and $\frac{1}{2}$ tsp sesame oil with 60ml vegetable or chicken stock. In large wok or frying pan, heat 1 tbsp groundnut oil over a medium heat. Add 3 lightly smashed garlic cloves and fry until lightly golden, then add a grated 3cm knob of fresh root ginger and fry for 30 seconds. Tip in the Chinese broccoli and stir-fry for 30 seconds. Pour in the sauce, put the lid on and let the vegetables steam for 2–3 minutes until the broccoli is tender. Serve immediately, with steamed rice. SERVES 4

Chinese **cabbage stir-fried** with **ginger**

Heat 1 tbsp groundnut oil in a wok. Add a grated 3cm knob of fresh root ginger and fry over a high heat for less than a minute until fragrant. Stir in 200g baby corn, halved lengthways, and 220g halved, tinned water chestnuts and fry for another minute. Add a thinly sliced $\frac{1}{2}$ head of Chinese cabbage, 4 sliced spring onions, 1 tbsp light soy sauce, 2 tbsp oyster sauce and 2 tsp sesame oil. Stir-fry for 2–3 minutes until the cabbage and corn are just tender. SERVES 4

Braised **pak choi**

Heat 1 tbsp each groundnut and sesame oils in a large sauté pan or wok over a medium heat. Add a grated 2.5cm knob of fresh root ginger and 2 finely chopped garlic cloves and fry, stirring, for about a minute until fragrant. Halve 450g pak choi lengthways and place in the pan, cut-side down. Fry for a minute or so, turning occasionally. Mix together 60ml chicken or vegetable stock, 1 tbsp light soy sauce, 1 tbsp dark soy sauce and 1 tbsp brown sugar and pour over the pak choi. Simmer for 3–5 minutes until the pak choi is tender, but retaining a slight crunch. Serve immediately. SERVES 4

Spicy Chinese **greens**

Cut 400g choi sum or pak choi leaves into thirds. Add to a pan of boiling water and blanch for 2–3 minutes until the leaves have just wilted, the stalks retaining a crunch. Drain, refresh in iced water and drain well. Heat 2 tbsp groundnut oil in a wok or sauté pan over a medium-high heat. Add 3 finely chopped garlic cloves and 2 finely sliced red chillies and fry for 30 seconds until fragrant. Add the blanched greens and toss well. Add 2 tbsp soy sauce, 1 tbsp oyster sauce and a grinding of white pepper. Stir-fry until the greens are piping hot. SERVES 4

Stir-fried Chinese **spinach**

Place a wok over a high heat and add $1\frac{1}{2}$ tbsp groundnut oil. When hot, add 3 finely chopped garlic cloves and toss for 30 seconds until lightly golden. Add 500g Chinese spinach and stir-fry for 1–2 minutes until the leaves are just wilted. Add 2 tsp spicy fermented bean paste, $1\frac{1}{2}$ tbsp oyster sauce and a good grinding of white pepper. Stir-fry until the greens are nicely coated in the sauce. Serve immediately. SERVES 4

Green beans and mushrooms in black bean sauce

THIS IS A QUICK, TASTY STIR-FRY of vegetables. Fermented black soy beans – sometimes labelled as salted black beans – are available from Asian grocers and selected supermarkets. They are, in fact, salted, fermented and dried beans, which may also be flavoured with chilli or ginger. They are normally rinsed before cooking to remove some of the excess salt.

SERVES 4

400g green beans, trimmed
225g shiitake mushrooms, cleaned
2 tbsp vegetable or groundnut oil
1 tbsp fermented black beans, rinsed and dried
2 large garlic cloves, peeled and chopped

Sauce:
2 tbsp Chinese rice vinegar
2 tbsp Shaoxing or Chinese rice wine (or dry sherry)
2 tbsp light soy sauce
1 tbsp oyster sauce
1 tsp caster sugar
1 tsp cornflour, mixed with 2 tbsp water

Cut the green beans into finger lengths and finely slice the mushrooms. Mix together all the ingredients for the sauce in a bowl and set aside.

Heat the oil in a wok over a medium-high heat. Tip in the black beans and garlic and fry for 30 seconds or so, until fragrant. Add the green beans with a little splash of water. Stir-fry for 2 minutes, then add the mushrooms. Stir-fry for another minute or two.

Pour the sauce over the vegetables and toss well. Simmer for a couple of minutes until the sauce begins to thicken and the green beans are tender but still retain a slight crunch. Transfer to a warm plate and bring to the table.

Cantonese fried rice

THIS IS A GREAT WAY TO USE UP LEFTOVER RICE – in fact it works better, as it is less sticky and easier to fry than freshly steamed rice. (Note, however, that leftover rice should be refrigerated and used within a day of cooking.) You can replace the prawns with diced chicken, roast pork or ham, and vary the vegetables – diced peppers, courgettes and sweetcorn all work well.

SERVES 4

100g raw prawns or shrimps, peeled
4 tbsp vegetable or groundnut oil
1 onion, peeled and chopped
2 large garlic cloves, peeled and finely chopped
1 carrot, peeled and diced
sea salt and white pepper
50g peas, thawed if frozen
2 medium eggs, beaten with a pinch of salt
about 400g day-old cooked rice
3–4 spring onions, trimmed and chopped
2 tbsp light soy sauce, or to taste

Devein the prawns, if using, and if they are quite large, roughly chop them; cover and set aside.

Heat half the oil in a wok over a medium-high heat. Add the onion, garlic, carrot and a pinch each of salt and pepper. Stir-fry for about 2–3 minutes until the vegetables begin to soften.

Tip in the prawns or shrimps and peas and stir-fry until the prawns begin to turn pink. Push the ingredients to one side of the wok and add a little more oil to the other. Add the beaten eggs to the oil and cook, stirring occasionally, to scramble them. Once they are almost set, stir them through the rest of the ingredients.

If necessary, add a little more oil to the wok and then tip in the rice and spring onions. Season with some soy sauce and stir-fry for 3–4 minutes until the rice is piping hot. Taste and adjust the seasoning before serving.

Fruit salad
with **star anise** syrup

A SIMPLE PLATTER OF FRESH FRUIT, such as sliced oranges, typically rounds off a Chinese meal. Following the same principle, this exotic fruit salad is a light and refreshing finale. There are no hard and fast rules – treat the selection below merely as a suggestion and adapt it to include any fruit in season.

SERVES 4

200g lychees
1 large ripe mango
1 star fruit, trimmed
1 large dragon fruit
2 persimmons

Star anise syrup:
75g caster sugar
juice of 1 lime
2 star anise
150ml water

To serve (optional):
few mint leaves, shredded
small handful of coriander leaves

First, make the star anise syrup. Put the sugar, lime juice, star anise and water into a saucepan and stir over a medium heat until the sugar dissolves. Increase the heat slightly and boil for 7–8 minutes until thickened to a light syrup. Take off the heat and leave to cool completely.

Prepare the fruit: peel and stone the lychees; peel, stone and slice the mango; slice the star fruit; cut the dragon fruit into wedges; peel the persimmons and cut into wedges.

Arrange the fruits attractively on a large platter and drizzle the star anise syrup over them (you may not need all of it; keep any extra in the fridge to drizzle over other fruit salads). Cover the platter with cling film and chill for 30 minutes before serving.

Scatter over the shredded mint and coriander leaves to serve, if using.

Wonton and sesame **twists** with sesame ice cream

THIS ICE CREAM MAY NOT LOOK INVITING, but it has a wonderfully intense sesame flavour. For a milder taste – and more enticing colour – use white, rather than black sesame seeds. The crispy wonton and sesame twists add an interesting texture, but if you haven't time to make them, serve dessert biscuits instead.

SERVES 4

Sesame ice cream:
85g black (or white) sesame seeds
4 large egg yolks
100g caster sugar
250ml whole milk
250ml double cream

Wonton and sesame twists:
8 wonton wrappers, thawed
    if frozen
1 medium egg, lightly beaten
1 tbsp black (or white) sesame
    seeds (or a combination)
vegetable or groundnut oil,
    for frying
icing sugar, to dust

To make the ice cream, toast the sesame seeds in a dry pan, tossing frequently, until fragrant and lightly golden. Tip onto a plate and leave to cool, then finely grind in a small food processor to a fine paste.

Beat the egg yolks and sugar together in a bowl until creamy. Put the milk and half of the cream into a heavy-based saucepan over a medium heat. Simmer gently for a minute, then whisk a little of the warm, creamy milk into the sugary yolks. Now gradually whisk this into the milk in the pan. Stir with a wooden spoon over a medium-low heat until the custard is thickened enough to lightly coat the back of the spoon.

Add the sesame paste to the hot custard. (For a smooth texture, press through a sieve.) Set over a bowl of iced water to cool quickly. In another bowl, whip the remaining cream to soft peaks, then fold through the cooled custard. Pour into an ice-cream machine and churn until almost frozen. Transfer to a suitable container and freeze until firm.

To make the wonton and sesame twists, cut each wonton wrapper into 4 long strips. Make a lengthways slit in the centre of each (like a button-hole) and push one end through to create a twist. Brush the twists with beaten egg and then lightly coat with sesame seeds. Lay on a board.

Heat a 3–4cm depth of oil in a wok or heavy-based deep saucepan until hot. Fry the twists in batches until crisp and golden brown all over, about 1–2 minutes on each side. Remove with a slotted spoon and drain on kitchen paper. Cool, then dust with icing sugar before serving.

To serve, place one or two scoops of sesame ice cream in each bowl and add a few sesame and wonton twists.

THAI

ABOVE ALL ELSE, THAI FOOD IS WONDERFULLY
FRAGRANT. THE USE OF INGREDIENTS, SUCH AS
LIMES, COCONUT, LEMONGRASS AND LIME LEAVES,
MAKES THE FOOD ENTICINGLY AROMATIC. IT CAN
SOMETIMES BE VERY FIERY, TOO, BUT ALWAYS FULL
OF FANTASTIC FLAVOURS. I SEE IT AS A VERY HEALTHY
FOOD AND IT HAS A REAL FEEL GOOD FACTOR WHEN
YOU EAT IT. AS WITH INDIAN FOOD THERE IS SO MUCH
MORE TO THAI COOKING THAN CURRIES. ONE WORD
OF ADVICE: NEVER SKIMP ON THE QUALITY OF THE
INGREDIENTS. THE KEY TO THAI FOOD IS FRESHNESS,
SO EVERYTHING MUST BE IN PEAK CONDITION.

Fishcakes with spicy cucumber relish

CURRIED PRAWN AND WHITE FISHCAKES are a real treat, but you do need to enjoy them freshly cooked, as they do not reheat well. Also, to ensure the patties have an interesting texture, it is important to avoid overblending the fish and prawn mixture.

MAKES 10–12

250g skinless white fish fillets, such as coley or ling
250g large prawns, peeled and deveined
1 tbsp Thai red curry paste
1 kaffir lime leaf, finely shredded (or finely grated zest of 1 lime)
1 tbsp chopped coriander
1 medium egg
1 tsp palm sugar (or brown sugar)
1 tsp fish sauce
pinch of sea salt
30g fine French beans, trimmed and thinly sliced
vegetable oil, for shallow-frying

Spicy cucumber relish:
1 cucumber
1/2 small red chilli, deseeded and thinly sliced
1 shallot, peeled and finely sliced
juice of 2 limes
2 tbsp caster sugar
1/2 tsp sea salt
2–3 tbsp water
small handful of coriander, leaves roughly chopped
small handful of mint, leaves roughly chopped

First, make the spicy cucumber relish. Peel the cucumber and quarter lengthways, then scoop out the seeds in the centre with a teaspoon. Thinly slice the cucumber on the diagonal and place in a large bowl. Add the chilli and shallot, toss to mix and set aside.

Put the lime juice, sugar, salt and water into a small saucepan and bring to a simmer, stirring well to dissolve the sugar. Let simmer for a few minutes until slightly thickened, then set aside to cool completely.

Put all the ingredients for the fishcakes, except the French beans and oil, into a food processor and pulse to a finely chopped wet paste. Do not overprocess, as you want to keep some texture to the fishcakes.

Scrape the mixture into a bowl and stir in the French beans. To check the seasoning, fry off a little ball of mixture in an oiled pan and taste, then adjust the seasoning of the uncooked mixture accordingly, adding a little more salt and/or sugar as necessary. With wet hands, shape the mixture into small patties about 5cm in diameter, each from about 2 tablespoonfuls of mixture.

Heat a 2–3cm depth of oil in a deep frying pan or wok. Fry the patties in batches for 1–2 minutes on each side, until golden brown. Drain on a tray lined with kitchen paper and keep warm in a low oven while you cook the rest.

When the fishcakes are all cooked, pour the dressing over the cucumber relish and stir in the chopped herbs. Serve the fishcakes hot, with the cucumber relish on the side.

Chicken in spicy coconut broth

THIS WONDERFULLY AROMATIC SOUP, called *tom ka gai*, is one of my favourite Thai starters. It is incredibly easy to make and cooks in next to no time. For a quick midweek supper, serve larger bowls – tossing in some blanched rice noodles and a handful of beansprouts and coriander leaves. Simple and delicious.

SERVES 4–6

2 boneless, skinless chicken breasts, about 250g
sea salt and black pepper
400ml tin reduced-fat coconut milk
600ml water
3cm knob of fresh root ginger, peeled and sliced
4 kaffir lime leaves, torn in half (or pared zest of 1 lime)
1 lemongrass stalk, trimmed and halved lengthways
2 red chillies, halved lengthways and deseeded
1 tbsp palm sugar (or soft light brown sugar)
2$^1\!/_2$ tbsp fish sauce
2 tbsp lime juice, or to taste
100g button mushrooms, cleaned
handful of coriander leaves, to garnish

Thinly slice the chicken breasts, cutting across the grain, into bite-sized pieces. Place in a bowl, season with a little salt and pepper and set aside.

Pour the coconut milk into a saucepan, then add the 600ml water, using the tin as a measure (i.e. 1$^1\!/_2$ tins). Add the ginger, kaffir lime leaves, lemongrass, chillies, sugar, fish sauce and lime juice. Bring to a simmer and cook gently, stirring occasionally, for about 5 minutes to allow the flavours to infuse.

Add the mushrooms to the broth and simmer for 2–3 minutes. Add the chicken, stir well and simmer until cooked through; this will only take 1–2 minutes. Taste and adjust the seasoning if you need to.

Serve the soup in warm bowls, discarding the ginger, lemongrass, chillies and lime leaves if you wish; traditionally, these aromatics are left in the soup but not eaten. Garnish each bowl with some coriander leaves and serve immediately.

Thai red curry paste

You will need 6–7 long, red chillies. To prepare, roll each chilli between your fingers to loosen the seeds, then cut off the stem end and squeeze out the seeds. Chop the chillies, then wash your hands thoroughly.

To make the red curry paste, put the chillies into a food processor with 4 chopped shallots, 5–6 chopped garlic cloves, a 4cm chopped knob of fresh root ginger, 1 trimmed and finely chopped lemongrass stalk, 1 finely chopped kaffir lime leaf (or the grated zest of 1 lime) and a handful of chopped coriander stems. Grind to a fine paste, adding 1–2 tbsp vegetable oil as necessary.

Grind 1 tsp each lightly toasted coriander and cumin seeds with $1^1/2$ tsp black peppercorns and 1 tsp sea salt to a fine powder, using a pestle and mortar. Tip this into the food processor and add 1 tsp shrimp paste, if you like. Blend until finely ground and well combined; you will need to stop the machine to scrape down the side of the bowl a few times to get an evenly ground wet paste. Store the curry paste in a screw-topped jar, refrigerate and use within a week. MAKES ABOUT 280g

Pork satay with peanut sauce

SATAY IS A POPULAR STREET FOOD in Thailand. I've used pork here, but it is also made with chicken, beef, squid and prawns. For optimum flavour, allow the pork plenty of time to marinate; this also helps to tenderise the meat. Satay is best cooked on the barbecue as it takes on a slightly smoky flavour, but you can, of course, use the grill or a griddle pan.

SERVES 4-6

500g pork loin or fillet
125ml tinned coconut milk
3cm knob of fresh root ginger, peeled and grated
1 lemongrass stalk, trimmed and white part finely chopped
1 tsp ground turmeric
2 tsp ground coriander
2 tsp ground cumin
1/2 tsp sea salt
freshly ground black pepper
1-2 tsp caster sugar
vegetable or groundnut oil, for brushing

Thai peanut sauce:
100g roasted skinned peanuts (unsalted)
200ml tinned coconut milk
4-5 tbsp Thai red curry paste (to make your own, see page 186)
1 1/2 tsp sea salt
1-2 tbsp palm sugar (or soft light brown sugar)
2-3 tbsp tamarind paste (or lime juice)

Slice the pork into long, thin strips across the grain. Mix the rest of the ingredients, except the oil, together in a large bowl, add the pork and toss to coat well. Cover with cling film and leave to marinate in the fridge for at least an hour, preferably overnight, to allow the flavours to develop. Soak 8-12 bamboo skewers in warm water (this will prevent them from scorching under the grill).

Meanwhile, make the peanut sauce. Pulse the peanuts in a food processor until very finely chopped (or coarsely ground), then tip into a bowl. Spoon the thick creamy layer of the coconut milk into a saucepan. Heat gently and when the oil separates from the milk, add the curry paste and cook until it is fragrant.

Now add the remaining coconut milk and the finely chopped peanuts. Stir in the salt, sugar and tamarind paste and simmer gently, stirring frequently, until the sauce thickens. (If the sauce is too thick, stir in a little boiling water.) Pour into a bowl and allow to cool completely.

Heat up the barbecue, grill or griddle pan. Thread the marinated pork slices onto the presoaked bamboo skewers. Brush with a little oil to prevent them from sticking and drying out and cook for 1 1/2-2 minutes on each side. Serve hot, with the peanut sauce for dipping.

Red snapper with chilli, tamarind and lime sauce

THIS IS MY TAKE ON A DISH I ENJOYED in Thailand several years ago – a whole crispy fried pomfret smothered in a delicious sweet, sour and hot tamarind sauce. Utterly divine. My healthier version uses red snapper fillets, but you can use any firm white fish for this recipe.

SERVES 4

4 red snapper fillets, about
   100–120g each
sea salt and black pepper
2 tbsp vegetable or groundnut oil
handful of baby spinach leaves
   (optional)

Sauce:
1$^1/_2$ tbsp vegetable or groundnut
   oil
4 long red chillies, deseeded and
   chopped
6 garlic cloves, peeled and
   chopped
4 spring onions, trimmed and
   finely sliced on the diagonal
2 tbsp lime juice
4 tbsp tamarind paste (or lime
   juice)
2 tbsp soy sauce
2 tbsp fish sauce
2 tsp palm sugar (or soft light
   brown sugar)
2 tbsp water

Check the fish fillets for small bones, removing any you find with kitchen tweezers. Set aside at room temperature while you prepare the sauce.

For the sauce, heat the oil in a saucepan over a medium heat. Add the chillies and garlic and cook, stirring frequently, for 1–2 minutes until fragrant. Add the rest of the ingredients, stir well and simmer gently for about 5–10 minutes until the sauce has reduced to a light jammy consistency. If it thickens too much, add a touch more water to thin it down slightly.

Season the red snapper fillets with salt and pepper. Heat the oil in a wide (preferably non-stick) frying pan. Fry the fish fillets, skin-side down, for 1$^1/_2$ minutes until the skin is lightly golden brown and the fish is cooked two-thirds of the way up. Flip the fish fillets over and cook the other side for about 30 seconds just until the flesh turns opaque and feels just firm.

To serve, spoon the sauce onto warm plates. If you wish, scatter over a layer of spinach leaves before arranging a fish fillet on each plate. Serve immediately, with plain jasmine rice.

Fragrant green curry with beef

YOU CAN USE ANY TENDER MEAT OR POULTRY, or firm-fleshed fish you fancy for this curry. The 'green' in the curry paste tends to become muted upon cooking, but the fragrance and flavours will intensify with heat. Use fewer chillies if you prefer a milder curry. You will have more green curry paste than you need for this recipe, but like the red curry paste (on page 186), it can be stored in a screw-topped jar in the fridge for up to a week.

SERVES 4

Green curry paste:
10 long, green chillies
3 shallots, peeled
6 garlic cloves, peeled
4cm knob of fresh root ginger, peeled
bunch of coriander, stems only
2 lemongrass stalks, trimmed
3 kaffir lime leaves (or finely grated zest of 2 limes)
1–2 tbsp vegetable oil
1 tbsp coriander seeds
1 tsp cumin seeds
1/2 tsp black peppercorns
1 tsp sea salt
1 tsp shrimp paste (optional)

Beef curry:
450g beef fillet or tenderloin
5 baby aubergines, (or 1 small regular one), trimmed
1 tbsp vegetable oil
400ml tin coconut milk
2 red chillies, halved lengthways
2 kaffir lime leaves, torn in half
11/2 tbsp fish sauce
1 tsp palm sugar (or brown sugar)
handful of shredded Thai sweet basil or coriander

First, make the curry paste. Roughly chop the green chillies, shallots, garlic, ginger and coriander stems and place in a food processor. Finely chop the lemongrass and lime leaves, add these to the processor and grind to a fine paste, adding 1–2 tbsp oil as necessary.

Toast the coriander and cumin seeds in a dry frying pan over a medium heat for about a minute until fragrant. Using a pestle and mortar, grind the toasted spices, peppercorns and salt to a fine powder. Tip this into the food processor and add the shrimp paste, if using. Blend until the mixture is well combined, stopping to scrape down the sides of the bowl a few times, to ensure an evenly ground wet paste.

To prepare the curry, slice the beef into bite-sized pieces and set aside. Similarly, cut the aubergines into bite-sized pieces and put to one side.

Heat the oil in a large pan or wok. Add 3–4 tbsp of the curry paste and stir over a medium heat until fragrant. Add the coconut milk and bring to a simmer. When the oil separates from the milk, add the aubergines, chillies, lime leaves, fish sauce and sugar. Cook for 3–4 minutes until the aubergines are tender, then add the beef and cook for another 2 minutes. Remove the pan from the heat.

Ladle the curry into warm bowls and scatter over the basil or coriander. Serve immediately, with steaming bowls of fragrant jasmine rice.

Stir-fried **chicken** with **cashew nuts**

NUTS ARE OFTEN ADDED TO THAI STIR-FRIES, just as they are to similar Chinese dishes. The important thing to remember when stir-frying is to have all the ingredients prepared and the vegetables chopped before you fire up the wok. Once you start cooking, it literally takes minutes to get the dish to the table.

SERVES 4

2–3 boneless, skinless chicken breasts, about 400g in total
sea salt and black pepper
2 tbsp vegetable or groundnut oil
50g cashew nuts
1 small onion, peeled and sliced
3 garlic cloves, peeled and chopped
1 dried red chilli, cut into 1cm pieces
3 spring onions, trimmed and cut on the diagonal into 3cm pieces
1½ tbsp fish sauce
1 tbsp dark soy sauce
pinch of caster sugar
1 red chilli, deseeded and sliced on the diagonal

Cut the chicken breasts into bite-sized pieces and mix with a pinch each of salt and pepper. Set aside.

Heat the oil in a wok or a wide frying pan. Add the cashew nuts and stir over a medium heat until toasted and lightly golden. Remove from the wok with a slotted spoon and set aside.

Add the onion and garlic to the wok and stir-fry for 3–4 minutes. Tip in the dried chilli, then add the chicken pieces. Stir-fry for 2 minutes until the chicken is opaque. Add the spring onions, fish sauce, soy sauce and a pinch of sugar and stir-fry for another minute. Finally, tip in the sliced red chilli and toasted cashew nuts. Stir well and turn off the heat.

Spoon the mixture onto a warm platter or divide between warm bowls and serve immediately, with freshly steamed jasmine rice.

Spicy stir-fried vegetables

USE ANY COLOURFUL COMBINATION of vegetables you fancy for this tasty dish. Just take care to avoid overcooking – the vegetables should be just tender but still retain a lovely crunch as you bite into them.

SERVES 4

1 large onion, peeled and sliced
1 medium carrot, peeled and sliced on the diagonal
2 garlic cloves, peeled and chopped
3cm knob of fresh root ginger, peeled and cut into matchsticks
100g shiitake mushrooms, cleaned and sliced
1 red pepper, cored, deseeded and cut into strips
1 small head of broccoli, trimmed and cut into tiny florets
3 spring onions, trimmed and cut into finger lengths
2 tbsp vegetable or groundnut oil

Sauce:
3 tbsp vegetable or chicken stock
2 tbsp fish sauce, or to taste
2 tbsp light soy sauce
1 tbsp lime juice, or to taste
1 tbsp runny honey (or caster sugar), or to taste
2 tsp cornflour, mixed with 3 tbsp water
pinch of dried chilli flakes

Have all the vegetables and aromatics prepared and ready to cook. In a bowl, mix together the ingredients for the sauce.

Place a wok or a wide frying pan over a medium heat. Add the oil and swirl it around the wok to coat. Add the onion and stir-fry for a minute. Add the carrot, garlic and ginger and stir-fry for another minute. Now add the mushrooms and stir-fry for another couple of minutes until the carrot begins to soften.

Tip the red pepper, broccoli and spring onions into the wok, then pour over the sauce. Stir-fry for another 2–3 minutes until the pepper and broccoli have both softened slightly but still retain a bite. Taste and adjust the seasoning, adding a little more fish sauce, lime juice or honey as needed.

Divide the stir-fry between warm plates or bowls and serve immediately.

Pad Thai with prawns

ONE OF THE MOST POPULAR DISHES on Thai restaurant menus, this isn't difficult to make at home. You just need to make sure that you don't overcrowd the wok. So, if you decide to increase the quantities here – to serve more guests – fry the noodles in batches, two portions at a time.

SERVES 2

125g thin or medium dried rice noodles

1¹/₂ tbsp caster sugar

2 tbsp fish sauce

2 tbsp tamarind paste (or lime juice)

4 tbsp vegetable oil

1 shallot, peeled and chopped

2 large garlic cloves, peeled and chopped

¹/₂ red chilli, deseeded and finely chopped

100g raw prawns, peeled and deveined

2 medium eggs

50g beansprouts

2 spring onions, trimmed, green part only, cut into finger lengths

3 tbsp roasted chopped peanuts, to sprinkle

lime wedges, to serve

Soak the rice noodles in boiling water for about 10 minutes until flexible and pliable but not overly soft, or cook according to the pack instructions. (Some dried noodles need to be blanched in boiling water for several minutes to soften them.)

Meanwhile, combine the sugar, fish sauce and tamarind paste in a small bowl and stir well. When ready, drain the noodles and set aside.

Heat half the oil in a wok or a large non-stick frying pan until hot. Add the shallot, garlic and chilli and stir over a medium heat until fragrant. Tip in the prawns and stir-fry for a couple of minutes until they turn orangey pink and opaque. Remove the prawns to a plate with a slotted spoon and set aside.

Drain the rice noodles and add to the wok with the sauce and a little splash of water. Stir-fry for a few minutes until they are tender. Push the ingredients in the wok to one side and add a little more oil to the other side. Crack the eggs over the oil and scramble lightly until they are almost cooked, then fold into the noodles.

Return the prawns to the wok and add the beansprouts and spring onions. Stir briefly over the heat, until the vegetables are slightly wilted but still crunchy.

Divide the pad Thai between warm shallow serving bowls and sprinkle with the chopped peanuts. Serve immediately, with lime wedges.

Banana fritters
with **sesame** seeds

I LIKE TO EAT THESE SWEET HOT FRITTERS with a scoop of contrasting cold, creamy vanilla ice cream. Pure indulgence. You do need to eat them fairly soon after cooking to enjoy them at their crispy best.

SERVES 6-8

5–6 large, firm but ripe bananas
vegetable or groundnut oil, for
    deep-frying
icing sugar, to dust

Batter:
2 tbsp desiccated coconut
100g rice flour
100g cornflour
4 tbsp sesame seeds
1 tsp fine sea salt
2 tbsp caster sugar
225–275ml water

First, prepare the batter. Put the desiccated coconut, rice flour, cornflour, sesame seeds, salt and sugar into a large bowl and stir well. Make a well in the centre of the dry ingredients and pour in the water. Stir until evenly blended and there are no lumps in the batter. It should be fairly thick.

About 10 minutes before you will be ready to serve, peel the bananas and cut each one into 3 or 4 short lengths. Heat a 5–6cm depth of oil in a wok or deep heavy-based saucepan until hot. To test if the oil is hot enough, drop a little batter into the pan – it should sizzle immediately.

Cook the fritters in batches. Dip the banana pieces in the batter to coat all over, then carefully lower into the hot oil. Fry for a few minutes until golden brown all over, turning once. Remove and drain on a plate lined with kitchen paper. Keep warm, while you cook the rest of the fritters.

Dust the crisp, hot fritters with icing sugar and serve straight away.

Mango, lime and coconut rice pudding

A LOVELY FRAGRANT RICE PUDDING that can be served hot or chilled if you prefer. If you decide to chill it, hold off preparing and adding the mango until you are ready to serve.

SERVES 4–6

250g jasmine rice
400ml tin coconut milk (reduced-fat, if preferred)
80g caster sugar
1 vanilla pod, slit in half lengthways
2–3 tbsp desiccated coconut
1 ripe mango
150ml double cream

To serve:
handful of pistachio nuts, chopped
1 lime, for zesting

Put the rice, coconut milk, sugar and vanilla pod into a saucepan. Bring to a simmer, stirring frequently, then cover the pan and cook for about 15–20 minutes until the rice is tender.

Meanwhile, lightly toast the coconut in a dry frying pan over a medium heat until golden brown, shaking the pan frequently. Tip onto a plate and leave to cool. Peel the mango and cut the flesh into chunks, away from the stone.

When the rice is ready, remove the pan from the heat and remove the vanilla pod. Stir in the toasted coconut, double cream and mango pieces until evenly combined. Cover again and allow to stand for 2–3 minutes.

Divide the rice pudding between serving bowls and scatter the chopped pistachios on top. Lightly grate over some lime zest and serve.

INDIAN

HAVING TRAVELLED EXTENSIVELY IN INDIA, I HAVE
COME TO APPRECIATE THE DIVERSITY OF THE FOOD. IT
ISN'T JUST DOWN TO THE GEOGRAPHY, THE DIFFERENT
RELIGIONS GOVERN WHAT INGREDIENTS ARE USED.
IN THE FAR NORTHEAST, PORK AND BEEF FEATURE IN
LOCAL DISHES, BUT THROUGHOUT MOST OF INDIA THE
COW IS CONSIDERED A SACRED ANIMAL AND NEVER
EATEN. IN GOA AND KERALA IN THE SOUTH, THE
COOKING HAS MORE OF A THAI FEEL, USING MILDER
SPICES AND COCONUT. THE NOTION THAT INDIAN FOOD
IS ALL ABOUT SLOPPY CURRIES THAT BLOW YOUR HEAD
OFF IS A LONG WAY FROM THE TRUTH, AS YOU'LL
DISCOVER FROM THE RECIPES IN THIS CHAPTER.

Prawn tandoori

A TANDOOR IS A DOME-SHAPED CLAY OVEN that is used in India to cook food at a very high temperature. Obviously, we can't replicate this in a domestic kitchen, but I find that a hot grill works perfectly for these marinated prawn skewers. They do not need long under the grill – just enough time to colour slightly around the edges.

SERVES 4

16 large prawns, peeled and deveined
2 tbsp lemon juice
1 tsp sea salt
2 tbsp vegetable oil
2 tbsp melted butter
lemon wedges, to serve

Marinade:
200g natural yoghurt
2 garlic cloves, peeled and crushed
2.5cm knob of fresh root ginger, peeled and grated
$1\frac{1}{2}$–2 tsp hot chilli powder
1 tsp paprika
1 tsp garam masala
1 tsp ajwain seeds, toasted
$\frac{1}{2}$ tsp sea salt

Wash the prawns and pat dry with kitchen paper. Place in a bowl with the lemon juice and salt and toss well to coat. Leave to marinate in the fridge for 15–20 minutes. If using bamboo skewers, soak four in warm water (this will prevent them from scorching under the grill).

Mix all the marinade ingredients together in a bowl. Drain the prawns, then place in a clean bowl and pour the marinade over them. Toss well to ensure they are coated all over, then cover and return to the fridge to marinate for $1\frac{1}{2}$–2 hours.

Preheat the grill to the highest setting. Mix the oil and melted butter together in a small bowl. Remove the prawns from the marinade and thread them onto the bamboo or metal skewers. Grill for 8–10 minutes, turning the skewers over and basting the prawns with the oil and butter mix halfway through cooking.

Serve the prawn skewers hot, with lemon wedges and a tomato and cucumber salad, if you wish.

Shaping
samosas

Shape each piece of samosa pastry into a ball, then roll out on a lightly floured surface to a circle, 12–15cm in diameter. Cut each in half to give 2 semi-circles. Working with one at a time, brush the edges with a little water, then fold the semi-circle in half to join the cut edges and form a cone shape. Press the dampened edges together to seal, then holding them together, open up the cone and spoon in some chickpea filling, to 1.5cm from the top. Brush the curved edges lightly with water and press these together to seal. Place on a tray lined with baking parchment. Repeat to make the rest of the samosas.

Curried chickpea **samosas**

TRADITIONALLY EATEN AS STREET SNACKS in India, samosas are now commonly served as a starter in restaurants. Usually they are deep-fried, although they can also be baked successfully with a generous brushing of melted butter. Samosas come with a variety of fillings, such as mixed vegetable, minced lamb, spicy potato and curried chickpeas, which I'm using here.

MAKES 12–16

Pastry:
225g plain flour, plus extra to dust
1$\frac{1}{2}$ tsp fine sea salt
1 tbsp melted butter (or oil)
5–6 tbsp warm water
vegetable oil, for deep-frying

Filling:
2 tbsp vegetable oil
1 tsp hot curry powder, or to taste
1 tsp garam masala
$\frac{1}{2}$ tsp ground cumin
$\frac{1}{2}$ tsp ground turmeric
1 small onion, peeled and finely chopped
1 garlic clove, peeled and finely chopped
2.5cm knob of fresh root ginger, peeled and grated
1 green chilli, deseeded and finely chopped
400g tin chickpeas, rinsed and drained
200ml water
$\frac{1}{2}$ tsp sea salt
100g peas, thawed if frozen, blanched if fresh
juice of $\frac{1}{2}$ lemon, or to taste

To make the pastry, combine the flour and salt in a large bowl. Make a well in the centre and add the melted butter and 5 tbsp warm water. Mix with a round-bladed knife to form a dough, adding another 1–3 tsp water if the mixture seems too dry. Tip onto a lightly floured surface and knead for 5–10 minutes to a smooth dough. Wrap in cling film and leave to rest in a cool part of the kitchen for at least 30 minutes.

For the filling, heat the oil in a wide frying pan or wok. Add the curry powder, garam masala, cumin and turmeric and cook, stirring, for 30 seconds. Next, add the onion, garlic, ginger and chilli and cook until the onion is softened and the spices are fragrant, about 4–5 minutes. Tip in the chickpeas, then add the water and salt. Cook, stirring gently, until most of the water has been absorbed, then take off the heat. Stir in the peas and lemon juice to taste. Transfer to a bowl and let cool completely.

Divide the pastry into 6 or 7 equal pieces. Now roll out the pastry and shape the samosas following my guide (on the preceding pages).

Heat a 6cm depth of oil in a deep heavy-based saucepan or wok over a medium heat to 180–190ºC. To test, drop a bread cube into the oil; it should sizzle on contact. Deep-fry the samosas in batches until golden brown and crisp, 6–8 minutes. Drain on a tray lined with kitchen paper and keep warm in a low oven while cooking the rest. Serve hot or warm.

Onion bhajis (top); samosas (left); spinach and potato cakes (right)

Onion bhajis
with spicy green sauce

THESE MILDLY SPICED ONION FRITTERS are customarily bound with gram flour, made from ground chickpeas, which is a good source of protein for the large vegetarian population in India. Gram flour is widely available at Asian groceries, but if you have difficulty sourcing it, simply replace with plain flour.

MAKES ABOUT 6

2 large onions, peeled and sliced
1/2 tsp sea salt, plus extra to sprinkle
1/2 tsp ground coriander
1/2 tsp cumin seeds
3–4 curry leaves, chopped
100g gram flour
75ml water
vegetable oil, for deep-frying

Spicy green sauce:
25g mint leaves
45g coriander leaves
1/2 garlic clove, peeled and very finely chopped
1–2 green chillies, to taste, deseeded and roughly chopped
1/2 tsp sea salt
1/2 tsp caster sugar
2 tsp lemon juice
about 125–150ml water

Sprinkle the onion slices with a little salt and set aside while you make the spicy green sauce (this helps to release some of their liquid).

To make the spicy green sauce, put the herbs, garlic, chilli(es), salt, sugar and lemon juice into a food processor. Blend, gradually adding the water through the feeder tube, until you have a fine wet paste, the consistency of a dipping sauce. Taste and adjust the seasoning, if required.

For the bhajis, mix the ground coriander, cumin, salt, curry leaves and gram flour together in a bowl. Squeeze the onions to get rid off the excess moisture (this will make it easier to bind the mix together and ensure that the bhajis are crisp once cooked). Add the onions to the spiced flour and toss well. Add the water, a little at a time, mixing well, until you have a thick batter that coats the onions.

Heat a 6cm depth of oil in a deep heavy-based saucepan or wok over a medium heat to 180–190°C. To test, drop a little of the batter into the oil; it should sizzle on contact. Drop spoonfuls of the batter into the hot oil, spacing them apart, and fry for 4–5 minutes, turning over halfway. When the bhajis are golden brown and crisp around the edges, remove them with a slotted spoon and drain on a tray lined with kitchen paper. Keep warm in a low oven while you fry the rest.

Serve the onion bhajis warm, with the spicy green sauce for dipping.

Illustrated on page 211

Spinach and potato cakes with cucumber raita

KNOWN AS *ALOO TIKKI*, these lovely patties originate from Lucknow, a region in India famed for its refined and exquisite food. The simple cucumber raita is a lovely accompaniment. You might also like to offer a contrasting tamarind or spicy green chutney.

MAKES 8–10 CAKES

2 medium potatoes, about 500g, peeled
sea salt and black pepper
3 tbsp vegetable oil, plus extra to fry the potato cakes
250g fresh spinach, washed
2 tsp black mustard seeds
1 tsp cumin seeds
2 garlic cloves, peeled and finely chopped
1 tsp fine sea salt, or to taste
1 tsp cayenne pepper
plain flour, to dust

Cucumber raita:
500ml plain yoghurt
1 large cucumber
1/2 tsp cumin seeds
1/2 tsp caster sugar

First, make the raita. Whisk the yoghurt briefly in a large bowl. Peel and grate the cucumber, then using your hands, squeeze out as much water as possible before adding to the yoghurt. Toast the cumin seeds in a dry frying pan for about a minute until fragrant, cool, then stir into the raita with the sugar. Season with salt and pepper to taste. Chill until ready to serve; the flavour will benefit if the raita is chilled for a few hours.

For the patties, cut the potatoes into large chunks and add to a pan of well-salted cold water. Bring to the boil and cook for 10–15 minutes until tender when pierced with a knife. Drain well and return to the heat briefly to dry the potato. While still hot, pass through a potato ricer into a bowl or mash smoothly. Season well to taste and leave to cool.

Heat a little oil in another large pan. Add the spinach and stir over a high heat until wilted. Tip into a colander and squeeze out excess moisture using the back of a ladle. Lay the leaves out on a tea towel, and again, squeeze out any moisture. Allow to cool, then chop the leaves coarsely.

Heat the remaining oil in a frying pan, add the mustard and cumin seeds and fry until they begin to splutter. Remove from the heat and add to the bowl of cooled mashed potato. Stir in the chopped spinach and season with salt and cayenne pepper. Shape the mixture into 8–10 balls and then flatten into small patties. Dust with a light coating of flour.

Heat a thin layer of oil in a wide (preferably non-stick) frying pan. When hot, fry the potato cakes in several batches for 2–3 minutes on each side until golden brown. Drain on kitchen paper, then serve warm with the cucumber raita on the side.

Illustrated on page 211

Keralan-style baked tilapia

THIS LOVELY FISH DISH TASTES FANTASTIC and takes little effort to prepare. Tilapia is an inexpensive, freshwater fish that is increasingly common at fishmongers and supermarket fish counters. However, if you can't find it, the spicy tomato mixture would work well with any firm, white fish fillets.

SERVES 4

4 tilapia fillets, about 130–150g
    each
sea salt and black pepper
2 tbsp vegetable oil
2 red onions, peeled and chopped
2 green chillies, deseeded and
    finely chopped
1 garlic clove, peeled and crushed
2cm knob of fresh root ginger,
    peeled and grated
1 tsp hot chilli powder
1 tsp ground coriander
3 large ripe tomatoes, finely
    chopped
juice of 1/2 lemon, or to taste
handful of coriander, leaves
    chopped
lemon wedges, to serve

Preheat the oven to 180°C/Fan 160°C/Gas 4. Check the fish for small bones, removing any with kitchen tweezers. Season the fillets with salt and pepper, then place in a single layer in a baking dish.

Heat the oil in a frying pan, add the onions and chillies and sauté over a medium heat for 4–5 minutes until softened but not coloured. Add the garlic, ginger, chilli powder and ground coriander and stir well. Cook for a few minutes until the oil separates out, then stir in the tomatoes. Season well and lower the heat slightly. Cook until the tomatoes are completely soft, then remove the pan from the heat and stir in the lemon juice and chopped coriander.

Spoon the spiced tomato mixture evenly over the fish fillets, making sure that they are completely covered. Bake in the oven for 10–15 minutes until the fish is just cooked – the flesh should feel firm when lightly pressed. Serve at once, with lemon wedges and steamed basmati rice.

Chicken Madras

THE UBIQUITOUS HOT CURRY on Indian restaurant menus. Typically, it is a fiery curry with a strong kick from both dried and fresh chillies. I've made my recipe a little milder, to cater for the palates of my young brood, but you can raise the heat by increasing the amount of chillies to taste.

SERVES 4

4 skinless, boneless chicken breasts, about 600g in total
3 tbsp vegetable oil
2 onions, peeled and finely chopped
2cm knob of fresh root ginger, peeled and grated
3 garlic cloves, peeled and finely chopped
2–3 green chillies, deseeded and finely chopped
2 tsp ground cumin
1 tsp ground coriander
1 tsp ground turmeric
1–1$\frac{1}{2}$ tsp hot chilli powder, to taste
6–8 curry leaves
sea salt and black pepper
400g ripe tomatoes, chopped
300ml water
1 tsp garam masala
coriander leaves, to garnish

Cut the chicken into 4cm pieces and set aside. Heat the oil in a wide saucepan or wok. Add the onions and cook until softened and lightly browned, about 6–8 minutes. Stir in the ginger, garlic and chillies and fry for 2–3 minutes. Add the cumin, coriander, turmeric, chilli powder and curry leaves and fry for a further minute. Season the chicken with salt and pepper and add to the pan. Fry, stirring, for 2–3 minutes on each side, until golden brown all over.

Tip the chopped tomatoes into the pan, pour in the water and bring to the boil. Stir well, lower the heat and put the lid on. Let simmer for 30 minutes, stirring occasionally. If the mixture becomes too dry and starts to stick to the bottom of the pan, add a little more water and stir well.

Stir in the garam masala and cook, uncovered, for a further 10 minutes. Serve garnished with coriander leaves and accompanied by pilau rice, plain basmati rice or warm Indian breads.

Lamb biryani

A BIRYANI IS A LAYERED DISH of rice and a vegetable or meat stew. Traditionally, the casserole is sealed with a simple flour and water pastry for the last stage of cooking. The dish is then brought to the table before the pastry lid is broken to unleash the fragrant aromas of the biryani. I've omitted the pastry to simplify the recipe, instead using a casserole dish with a well-fitting lid.

SERVES 4–5

750g boned lamb shoulder
2 onions, peeled and roughly chopped
5 garlic cloves, peeled
2.5cm knob of fresh root ginger, peeled
50g flaked almonds
3 tbsp water
6 tbsp vegetable oil
sea salt and black pepper
300ml water
1 tsp cumin seeds
1 tsp coriander seeds
1 cinnamon stick
1/2 tsp cardamom seeds
1 tsp black peppercorns, freshly ground

Fragrant rice:
400g basmati rice
2 tbsp unsalted butter
1/2 tsp ground turmeric
4 bay leaves
4 cloves
1 star anise
475ml water

Cut the lamb into 2cm cubes and set aside. Put the onions into a blender with the garlic, ginger, almonds and water and blitz to a paste. Heat 2–3 tbsp oil in a wide pan or wok and fry the lamb in batches until lightly browned all over, transferring the pieces to a bowl as they are ready.

When all the meat is browned, add a little more oil the pan and tip in the wet garlic, ginger and almond paste. Fry for 3–4 minutes, stirring constantly, until light brown in colour. If the paste begins to stick during this time, add a splash of water. Return the meat to the pan, season with salt and pepper and pour in the water. Partially cover the pan with the lid and simmer, stirring occasionally, for an hour.

Toast the cumin and coriander seeds in a dry frying pan for about a minute until fragrant. Grind the toasted seeds, cinnamon, cardamom and peppercorns together in a spice grinder. Stir this into the simmering meat and cook for a further 20–30 minutes until the meat is tender.

Preheat the oven to 180°C/Fan 160°C/Gas 4. To prepare the rice, wash it in several changes of cold water, then drain well. Heat the butter in a large saucepan and add the turmeric, bay leaves, cloves and star anise. When they begin to sizzle and smell fragrant, tip the drained rice into the pan and stir well to coat the grains in the butter. Cover with the water, bring to the boil and allow to cook for 10 minutes.

Spread the rice in a large, ovenproof casserole (that has a well-fitting lid) and spoon the lamb stew on top. Put the lid on and cook in the oven for 30–35 minutes. Turn off the oven and leave the biryani inside to stand for 10 minutes before serving.

Dhal

SPICY STEWED LENTILS or dhal is a staple with most Indian meals and is typically eaten as a side dish with rice or bread. The choice of dried pulses and spices varies from region to region. This dhal is made with yellow split lentils, called *tuvar dhal* – one of the more popular pulses in India. If you can't find it, substitute yellow split peas, mung beans or red lentils, presoaking as necessary and adjusting the cooking time accordingly.

SERVES 4

350g yellow split lentils

1 litre water

2 curry leaves

2 tomatoes, chopped

1 tsp ground turmeric

1 1/2–2 tsp hot chilli powder, to taste

1 tsp sea salt

30g unsalted butter

1 tsp panch phoran (Indian blend of 5 spices)

8 curry leaves

2 green chillies, slit in half lengthways

Wash the lentils thoroughly in several changes of cold water, then tip into a large saucepan and pour on the water to cover. Add the curry leaves, chopped tomatoes, turmeric, chilli powder and salt. Stir well, bring to the boil and then lower the heat. Skim off the froth and scum from the surface, then leave to simmer for 20–30 minutes until the lentils are soft. The dhal should have a thick soup-like consistency; if it is too thick, add some more warm water.

Reheat the lentils when you are ready to serve. Melt the butter in a frying pan. Add the panch phoran and the curry leaves and fry for a minute or so until they release their aroma. Add the green chillies and fry for a few more minutes.

Transfer the lentils to a warm serving bowl and tip the aromatic spice mix on top. Serve at once, with steamed basmati rice or warm Indian breads.

Cinnamon **kulfi**

COMPRISING ONLY THREE INGREDIENTS – reduced milk, sugar and natural flavouring in the form of cinnamon – this is a wonderfully simple kulfi recipe. I like to freeze the mixture in lolly moulds to amuse the kids, but you can also use the more traditional conical kulfi moulds, or French dariole moulds, depending on what you have to hand.

MAKES ABOUT 16

2 litres whole milk
3 cinnamon sticks
130g granulated sugar

Pour the milk into a large heavy-based saucepan and slowly bring to the boil. Turn down the heat, add the cinnamon sticks and simmer until reduced by half. This will probably take about an hour, during which time the milk needs to be stirred frequently to prevent it catching on the bottom of the pan. If a skin forms over the milk, just stir it back in.

When the milk has sufficiently reduced, add the sugar and stir well to dissolve. Cook for a further 2–3 minutes, then remove the pan from the heat and set aside to cool.

Once the liquid has cooled completely, remove the cinnamon sticks. Pour the mixture into ice-lolly moulds, or special kulfi or dariole moulds, and freeze overnight.

About 20 minutes before you wish to serve them, remove the kulfi from the freezer to allow them to soften slightly. When ready to serve, dip the moulds briefly in warm water to loosen them and unmould the kulfi.

Carrot and coconut halwa

HALWAS VARY SIGNIFICANTLY IN TEXTURE. Some recipes produce a soft pudding, but I prefer to cook the mixture until it is sticky and thick enough to be rolled into balls, which I coat with toasted desiccated coconut. I also add some chopped pistachios and almonds to the carrot mixture for a slightly nutty texture. Serve with coffee, or as a dessert or teatime treat.

MAKES 18–20

2kg carrots, peeled
500ml evaporated milk
500g granulated sugar
50g unsalted butter
2 cardamom pods, seeds extracted and finely crushed
25g toasted pistachio nuts, finely chopped
25g toasted almonds, finely chopped
50g desiccated coconut, lightly toasted

Coarsely grate the carrots and put them into a large heavy-based saucepan with the evaporated milk and granulated sugar. Bring to the boil and then lower the heat to a simmer. Cook for 35–45 minutes, stirring frequently, until all the milk has evaporated and the carrot is quite dry.

Add the butter to the saucepan and increase the heat slightly to roast the grated carrots. Cook for a further 25–30 minutes, stirring frequently, until the mixture is dry. When it leaves the sides of the pan clean, take off the heat and stir in the crushed cardamom seeds and chopped nuts.

Transfer the mixture to a wide dish and leave to cool completely, then chill for at least an hour to allow it to firm up more.

With wet hands, roll the mixture into neat round balls, then roll each ball in the toasted coconut to coat all over. The halwa are now ready to serve. They will keep in a sealed container in the fridge for up to a week.

AMERICAN

WELL WHAT CAN I SAY ABOUT AMERICAN FOOD? GUTSY AND GENEROUS, IT'S NOT FOR THE FAINT-HEARTED, BUT THAT'S NOT TO SAY THAT ALL AMERICAN FOOD IS RICH AND HEAVY. I SPEND A LOT OF TIME IN LOS ANGELES. WE HAVE A RESTAURANT IN THE CITY, AND ANOTHER OVER IN NEW YORK. AS WITH MOST VAST COUNTRIES, THE FOOD VARIES A LOT DEPENDING ON WHERE YOU ARE. NEW YORK, FOR EXAMPLE, IS MUCH MORE EUROPEAN IN ITS APPROACH TO COOKING COMPARED TO OTHER STATES. I WOULD CERTAINLY RECOMMEND THE BUFFALO CHICKEN WINGS – THEY ARE FANTASTIC – AND THE PUDDINGS ARE TO DIE FOR...

Maryland **crabcakes**

MARYLAND IS FAMOUS FOR ITS SUPERB CRABCAKES. They are seasoned with the distinctive flavours of Old Bay spice blend, which is produced by McCormick's and available online from specialist suppliers. If you can't source it, make a simple version using equal amounts of ground bay leaf, mustard seeds, black pepper, ginger, cinnamon and celery salt. Make extra, store in an airtight jar and use to sprinkle onto other seafood dishes.

SERVES 6–8

500g white crabmeat
1 small onion, peeled and finely chopped
1 celery stick, trimmed and finely chopped
1 tbsp Dijon mustard
1 tbsp mayonnaise
1 tsp Worcestershire sauce
1 medium egg, lightly beaten
1 tsp chopped flat-leaf parsley
1 tbsp Old Bay seasoning
about 50g fresh white breadcrumbs
vegetable or groundnut oil, for frying

To serve:
mayonnaise
lemon wedges
salad leaves

Pick over the crabmeat and discard any fragments of shell. Put the onion, celery, mustard, mayonnaise, Worcestershire sauce, beaten egg and chopped parsley into a bowl and mix well. Add the crabmeat and Old Bay seasoning and mix until evenly combined. Finally, incorporate 3–4 tbsp of the breadcrumbs – enough to obtain a firm mixture.

Cover with cling film and chill for at least 30 minutes to allow the mixture to firm up slightly.

With damp hands, shape the mixture into 6 or 8 neat patties. Heat a thin layer of oil in a large frying pan over a medium heat. Fry the patties for about 2–3 minutes on each side, until golden brown. Remove and drain on kitchen paper.

Serve the crabcakes hot with mayonnaise, lemon wedges and salad leaves.

New England
clam chowder

REGARDED AS ONE OF THE GREAT AMERICAN SOUPS, this is rich and creamy, with a delectable savoury flavour from the bacon and clams. The traditional garnish is oyster crackers. In San Francisco, clam chowder is sometimes served in hollowed-out sourdough bread bowls, as a sustaining lunch.

SERVES 4–6

1kg live clams, cleaned

splash of dry white wine

1 tbsp olive oil

100g maple-cured bacon, cut into strips

2 onions, peeled and finely chopped

2 celery sticks, trimmed (any leaves reserved) and finely chopped

3 large floury potatoes, about 600g, peeled and finely diced

1 garlic clove, peeled and chopped

30g butter

2^1/$_2$ tbsp plain flour

500ml chicken stock

200ml double cream

2 tbsp celery leaves, chopped (optional)

1 bay leaf

sea salt and black pepper

handful of flat-leaf parsley, leaves torn

Heat a large heavy-based saucepan until hot. Tip in the clams, add a splash of wine and cover the pan with a tight-fitting lid. Give it a shake and let the clams steam for 3–4 minutes until the shells have opened.

Tip the clams into a colander set over a large bowl to collect the juices. When cool enough to handle, shell most of the clams, leaving some in their shells for an attractive presentation; discard any that remain closed.

Heat the olive oil in a frying pan, add the bacon and fry for 3–4 minutes, or until crisp. Add the onions, celery, potatoes and garlic to the pan and fry gently for 6–8 minutes until starting to soften.

Add the butter, then the flour and cook, stirring, for a couple of minutes. Gradually add the stock to the pan, stirring constantly. Pour in the cream and the reserved juices from the clams. Add the chopped celery leaves, if available, bay leaf and seasoning. Bring to a simmer and cook for 20–30 minutes until the vegetables are soft and the chowder is thick.

Add all of the clams and warm through over a low heat, stirring, for 2–3 minutes; do not allow to boil. Ladle into warm bowls and serve, sprinkled with parsley.

Buffalo chicken wings with sour cream and chive dip

ALSO CALLED HOT WINGS, these feature on many American bar menus, as they are excellent finger food to be enjoyed with a cold beer. The crispy wings have a fiery kick from a liberal coating of hot sauce, so they are usually served with a contrasting and cooling soured cream or blue cheese dip and a handful of celery sticks.

SERVES 4–5

3–4 tbsp plain flour
1 tsp paprika
pinch of cayenne pepper, or
    to taste
sea salt
10 chicken wings
50g unsalted butter
4 tbsp hot sauce (such as Frank's
    Red-Hot Original Cayenne
    Pepper Sauce)
1/4 tsp black pepper
1 garlic clove, peeled and finely
    crushed
vegetable or groundnut oil, for
    deep-frying
lemon wedges, to serve

Sour cream and chive dip:
150ml soured cream
3–4 tbsp mayonnaise
handful of chives, finely chopped
sea salt and black pepper
1 tsp lemon juice, or to taste

In a small bowl, mix together the flour, paprika, cayenne pepper and a large pinch of salt. Put the chicken wings into a large bowl. Sprinkle the spiced flour mixture over them and toss well until evenly coated, then cover and refrigerate for about an hour.

Meanwhile, put the butter, hot sauce, pepper, garlic and a pinch of salt into a small saucepan over a low heat. Stir together and heat until the butter is melted and the mixture is well blended. Set aside to cool.

Meanwhile, for the dip, mix all the ingredients together in a small bowl, adding salt, pepper and lemon juice to taste. Cover and chill until you are ready to cook the chicken wings.

Heat a 6–7cm depth of oil in a deep-fryer or a heavy-based deep pan to 180ºC; a piece of bread dropped into the hot oil should sizzle on contact. Deep-fry the coated chicken wings in batches for 10–15 minutes, or until they begin to brown and crispen, turning them over halfway. Drain on a tray lined with kitchen paper and keep warm while you fry the rest.

Put the crispy wings into a large bowl, pour over the hot sauce mixture and stir until well coated.

Immediately arrange the buffalo wings on a warm platter or in individual bowls and serve with lemon wedges and the sour cream and chive dip.

Louisiana **seafood gumbo**

THIS MIXED SEAFOOD STEW is popular across the southern states. To keep it simple, I've limited the main ingredients to chorizo, crabmeat and oysters, however, recipes often feature prawns, crab, crayfish and smoked pork or andouille sausages – feel free to add any of these. Sometimes, instead of a roux, either sliced okra or filé powder (a spice made from ground dried sassafras leaves) is used to thicken the stew.

SERVES 4

6 tbsp vegetable oil
5 tbsp plain flour
2 large onions, peeled and chopped
4 celery sticks, trimmed and chopped
2 red peppers, cored, deseeded and chopped
4 garlic cloves, peeled and chopped
225g chorizo (or andouille) sausage, sliced
800ml fish or chicken stock
400g white crabmeat (or cooked crab claws)
6–7 spring onions, trimmed and chopped
pinch of cayenne pepper
sea salt and black pepper
12 live oysters
handful of flat-leaf parsley, chopped

Heat the oil in a large, wide pan over a medium-high heat. Sprinkle in the flour and cook, stirring, until the mixture turns golden brown (forming a brown roux).

Tip in the onions, celery, red peppers and garlic. Cook, stirring frequently, for about 8–10 minutes or until the vegetables are soft. Add the chorizo and cook for another 2–3 minutes.

Gradually add the stock to the pan, a ladleful at a time, stirring continuously. Let the mixture simmer, stirring often, for about 30 minutes until the stock is thick and flavourful, and the vegetables are soft.

Add the crabmeat, spring onions, cayenne and salt and pepper to the pan and stir well. Finally, shuck the oysters and tip them into the pan, along with their strained juices. Simmer for a couple of minutes, then turn off the heat.

Ladle the gumbo into warm bowls and scatter over the chopped parsley. Serve at once, with plain rice.

Chicken pot pie

MUCH LIKE THE BRITISH VERSION but with a lighter sauce, this classic American pie is terrific winter comfort food. Traditionally, a whole chicken is poached until tender, then the poaching liquor is reduced to make a flavourful stock for the pie. My simplified, but no less delicious, version uses tender chicken breasts; alternatively you could use leftover chicken from a previous night's roast.

SERVES 4

50g butter
1 large onion, peeled and chopped
3 celery sticks, trimmed and diced
1 large carrot, peeled and chopped
1 large potato, peeled and diced
50g plain flour, plus extra to dust
500ml chicken stock
250ml single cream
sea salt and black pepper
500g skinless, boneless chicken breasts, cut into bite-sized pieces
300g good-quality ready-made all-butter puff pastry
1 medium egg mixed with 1 tbsp water (egg wash), to glaze

Melt the butter in a large, wide pan and add the onion, celery, carrot and potato. Sauté gently for 10 minutes or until the vegetables are soft. Add the flour and stir well. Cook, stirring frequently, for another 2 minutes to cook out the flour.

Pour in the stock and cream and season well with salt and pepper. Bring to a simmer and cook, stirring, for about 5–10 minutes until thickened. Add the chicken and simmer for 5 minutes or until the pieces are just cooked through. Taste and adjust the seasoning. Take the pan off the heat and leave to cool slightly.

Preheat the oven to 200°C/Fan 180°C/Gas 6. Spoon the chicken filling into one large or 4 individual pie dish(es) to fill to just below the rim(s). Roll out the puff pastry on a lightly floured surface to a large round, the thickness of a £1 coin. Cut out a circle (or 4 small ones) large enough to form pie lid(s).

Re-roll the trimmings and cut long strips to fit around the rim of the dish(es). Brush the rim(s) with water, position the pastry strips and brush these with egg wash. Lift the pastry lid on top and crimp the edges to seal. If you wish, decorate the top of the pie with leaves cut from the pastry trimmings. Brush the pastry with egg wash to glaze.

Bake the pie in the oven for 40–50 minutes or until the pastry is golden brown and the filling is bubbling hot. Leave to stand for a few minutes before serving.

Blue cheese burgers

THE ADDITION OF CRUMBLY BLUE CHEESE gives these home-made burgers a lovely savoury edge. They take little time and effort to make and taste far superior to commercially made burgers. Baked sweet potato wedges and coleslaw (see page 243) are ideal accompaniments.

SERVES 6–8

Burgers:
1kg lean beef mince
1 small red onion, peeled and
    finely chopped
100g blue cheese, crumbled
small bunch of chives, chopped
few dashes of Tabasco sauce
2 tsp Worcestershire sauce
1 tsp English mustard
sea salt and black pepper
olive oil, to drizzle

To serve:
6–8 soft burger buns, split
handful of salad leaves
sliced tomatoes
sliced avocado
mayonnaise and/or tomato
    ketchup

To prepare the burgers, put all the ingredients, except the oil, into a large bowl, seasoning well with salt and pepper. Mix until well combined, using your hands. Break off a small piece of the mixture, shape into a ball and fry in an oiled pan until cooked, then taste for seasoning. Adjust the seasoning of the uncooked mixture as necessary. Cover the bowl with cling film and chill for a few hours.

Preheat a griddle pan or heat up the barbecue. With wet hands, shape the burgers into 6–8 neat patties. Brush or drizzle the patties with a little olive oil and cook for about 7–10 minutes, turning them over halfway through cooking. They should still be slightly pink in the centre.

When the burgers are almost ready, drizzle the cut side of the burger buns with a little olive oil. Toast the buns, cut-side down, on the barbecue or griddle until lightly golden.

To serve, sandwich the burger patties between the buns with some salad leaves, tomato and avocado slices, and a dollop of mayonnaise and/or ketchup, as you prefer.

5 ways with steak

Classic **steak tartare**

Finely dice 400g fillet steak. In a bowl, whisk 2 egg yolks with 1 tbsp Worcestershire sauce and a pinch of cayenne pepper. Add the steak along with 2 finely chopped gherkins, 1 chopped shallot, 1 tbsp Dijon mustard, 2 finely chopped anchovy fillets and a handful of chopped flat-leaf parsley. Season with sea salt and black pepper and mix well. Shape the beef into patties and serve on pumperknickel bread or with chips. SERVES 4

Skirt or flank **steak** with **chimichurri sauce**

For the sauce, mix 2 generous handfuls each of chopped coriander and parsley with 1 crushed garlic clove, 1 tbsp white wine vinegar, a squeeze of lemon juice and 100ml olive oil. Score the surface of an 800g piece skirt or flank steak against the grain and cut into 4 pieces. Lay in a dish, spoon on a third of the sauce and leave to marinate in the fridge for at least 2 hours, overnight if possible. Heat the grill to maximum or set a griddle pan over a high heat. Remove the steak from the marinade, brush off excess and season both sides with sea salt and black pepper. Grill or griddle for 2–3 minutes each side. Serve the steaks topped with the remaining sauce. SERVES 4

Peppered steak with **truffle** creamed **mushrooms**

Heat 1 tbsp olive oil in a pan and gently sauté 1 finely chopped onion and 1 finely chopped garlic clove until softened but not coloured. Add another 1 tbsp oil, a knob of butter and 200g sliced mixed mushrooms and cook until browned. Pour in 50ml white wine and let bubble until quite dry. Add 1 tsp truffle oil, 1 tsp finely chopped black truffle (if available) and 300ml double cream. Leave to simmer while you cook the steaks. Crush 40g black peppercorns and scatter on a plate. Season four 250g boneless rib eye steaks all over with sea salt, then press both sides into the crushed peppercorns. Place a heavy-based frying pan over a high heat and add 2 tbsp olive oil. When the pan is really hot, fry the steaks for 3 minutes on each side. The steaks should feel slightly springy for medium rare. Rest for a few minutes before serving, with the truffle creamed mushrooms. SERVES 4

Rump steak with **beer** and **onion** gravy

Season 4 rump steaks, about 250g each, on both sides with sea salt and black pepper. Melt 20g butter in a large frying pan over a medium heat. When the pan is really hot, add the steaks and cook for 3–4 minutes on each side for medium rare. Transfer to a warm plate, cover with foil and keep warm in a low oven while you make the gravy. Add another knob of butter to the pan along with 3 finely sliced onions and 2 tsp caster sugar. Cook over a medium-high heat until golden brown and caramelised. Add 1 tsp flour and cook for 1 minute, then stir in 200ml beer and 300ml beef stock. Let bubble for 8–10 minutes until thickened. Place each steak on a warm plate and spoon over the beer and onion gravy. SERVES 4

Chargrilled **steak** with **tomato** and **herb butter**

For the butter, blend 100g drained sun-dried tomatoes, 1 chopped garlic clove and 1 chopped shallot in a blender or food processor until smooth. Add 150g softened unsalted butter and a handful of chopped flat-leaf parsley and chives. Blend again briefly, then scrape out onto a piece of cling film and roll tightly in the film to form a cylinder, 3cm in diameter. Chill until ready to serve. Place a griddle pan over a high heat until smoking hot. Lightly brush 4 sirloin steaks, about 250–300g each, with olive oil and season on both sides with sea salt and black pepper. Griddle for 3 minutes on each side for medium rare. Transfer to warm plates and leave to rest for a few minutes. Top each steak with a couple of slices of herb butter to serve. SERVES 4

Barbecued short ribs
with coleslaw

BARBECUED RIBS ARE A GREAT CHOICE if you are feeding a crowd. I slow-cook them in a flavourful braising liquor beforehand so that they only need a few minutes on the barbecue. The rich, sticky barbecue glaze imparts a superb flavour. Of course, you can easily scale down the recipe to serve 4, 6 or 8.

SERVES 12

6 racks of pork spareribs, each
   with 6–7 ribs
3 tbsp tomato purée
2 onions, peeled and quartered
4 garlic cloves, lightly smashed
3/4 tsp black peppercorns
5 cloves
2 dried red chillies
sea salt and black pepper

For the barbecue glaze:
4 tbsp dark molasses
2 onions, peeled and finely
   chopped
4 tbsp runny honey
4 tbsp Worcestershire sauce
2 tbsp tomato purée
2 tbsp English mustard
2 tbsp cider vinegar
few good dashes of Tabasco sauce
juice of 1 lemon

Coleslaw:
1 small white cabbage, trimmed
4 large carrots, peeled and grated
8–10 tbsp mayonnaise
4 tbsp grainy mustard
2 tbsp lemon juice
2–3 tsp caster sugar

First, braise the ribs – you'll need a saucepan in which they will fit snugly (divide each rack in half if it's easier). Pour about 2 litres water into the pan and add the tomato purée, onions, garlic, peppercorns, cloves and dried chillies. Bring to the boil and let it bubble rapidly for 15 minutes. Add the rib racks and some seasoning. Top up with more water as necessary to ensure the ribs are covered and bring back to a gentle simmer. Skim off any scum or froth from the surface of the liquid. Simmer for about 45–60 minutes until the meat on the ribs is tender, adding more water during cooking if it reduces too much. Remove the pan from the heat and set aside to cool.

For the glaze, strain the braising liquor through a fine sieve into another pan and boil steadily until reduced by two-thirds. Add the molasses, onions, honey, Worcestershire sauce, tomato purée, mustard, cider vinegar, Tabasco, lemon juice and some salt and pepper. Stir over a high heat for 6–8 minutes, until the mixture begins to bubble and is syrupy.

For the coleslaw, finely shred the white cabbage and toss in a large bowl with the grated carrots. For the dressing, mix the mayonnaise, mustard, lemon juice and caster sugar together, then add to the cabbage mix. Toss well and season with salt and pepper to taste. Cover and chill until ready to serve.

Prepare the barbecue and let the fire burn down to grey embers. Alternatively, preheat a griddle pan until hot.

When ready to serve, brush the glaze liberally over the ribs then barbecue or griddle for 1½–2 minutes on each side (also illustrated overleaf). Serve with the coleslaw and crusty bread.

Boston cream pie

FILLED WITH CUSTARD – NOT CREAM,
as the name suggests – this heavenly sandwich
cake is topped with a rich chocolate frosting. It was
invented in Boston's historic Parker House Hotel,
where it still features on the restaurant menu.
My recipe makes a large cake, ideal for entertaining
a crowd, but if you have any left over it can be kept
in the fridge and eaten the next day.

SERVES 10–12

200g unsalted butter, softened,
    plus extra for greasing
450g plain flour, plus extra to dust
4 tsp baking powder
pinch of fine sea salt
300g caster sugar
2 tsp vanilla extract
4 large eggs, at room temperature,
    lightly beaten
225ml whole milk

Custard cream filling:
200ml double cream
50g caster sugar
pinch of fine sea salt
75ml whole milk
1 tbsp cornflour
2 large eggs
1 tsp dark rum (or vanilla extract)

Chocolate frosting:
85g good-quality dark chocolate,
    chopped
30g butter
60ml single cream
60g icing sugar
1 tsp vanilla extract

Preheat the oven to 180°C/Fan 160°C/Gas 4. Line two 23cm cake tins
with removable bases, then butter lightly and dust with flour.

Sift the flour, baking powder and salt together into a large bowl. Beat the
butter and sugar together in another large bowl until light and fluffy. Add
the vanilla extract, then gradually beat in the eggs. Fold in the flour
mixture, alternately with the milk.

Divide the mixture evenly between the prepared tins and gently level the
surface with a spatula. Bake for 20–30 minutes until a skewer inserted
into the centre comes out clean. Leave in the tins for 5 minutes or so, to
cool slightly, then turn the cakes out onto wire racks to cool completely.

For the filling, heat the cream in a heavy-based saucepan over a medium
heat until bubbles begin to form around the edge of the pan. Immediately
add the sugar and salt, stirring until dissolved. Take off the heat. In
a bowl, whisk the milk with the cornflour until smooth, then beat in the
eggs. Gradually pour this onto the hot cream mixture in a thin stream,
whisking constantly. Stir over a low heat until the custard is quite thick
and smooth, about 5 minutes. Take off the heat and stir in the rum. Leave
to cool completely, stirring occasionally to prevent a skin from forming.

For the frosting, stir the chocolate, butter and cream in a heavy-based
saucepan over a low heat until melted and smooth. Remove from the heat
and beat in the icing sugar and vanilla. Leave to cool, stirring occasionally.

To assemble the cake, spread the cooled filling over one of the cakes and
place the other cake on top. Pour the chocolate frosting evenly over the
top allowing it to drip slightly down the sides. Cut into slices to serve.

Deep-dish cherry pie

THIS IS THE QUINTESSENTIAL AMERICAN DESSERT. Like apple pie, it is a big favourite in diners and casual eateries across the country. The best way to enjoy it is with a large scoop of vanilla ice cream.

SERVES 6–8

Sweet pastry:

125g unsalted butter, softened
    to room temperature
90g caster sugar, plus extra
    to dust
1 large egg
250g plain flour, plus extra to dust
1–3 tsp ice-cold water (if needed)
1 medium egg, beaten with 1 tbsp
    water, to glaze

Filling:

1kg ripe cherries, pitted
100g caster (or vanilla) sugar
3 tbsp cornflour
25g butter, diced

To make the sweet pastry, whiz the butter and sugar together in a food processor until just combined. Add the egg and whiz for 30 seconds. Tip in the flour and process for a few seconds until the dough just comes together, adding a little water if needed. Knead lightly on a floured surface. Shape into a disc, wrap in cling film and chill for 30 minutes.

Divide the pastry into two pieces, one twice the size of the other. Roll out the larger portion on a lightly floured surface to the thickness of a £1 coin. Use it to line a 23cm deep pie dish, trimming off the excess pastry around the edge. Chill for 30 minutes.

Preheat the oven to 220°C/Fan 200°C/Gas 7. For the filling, toss the cherries in a bowl with the sugar and cornflour, then scatter evenly over the base of the pie. Dot the butter all over the cherry filling. Lightly brush the pastry rim with a little egg glaze.

Roll out the remaining pastry and cut into long strips, about 1cm wide. Arrange the strips on top of the pie in a lattice pattern, trimming off any excess pastry overhanging the edges. Brush the lattice with egg glaze and sprinkle lightly with caster sugar.

Bake in the hot oven for 10 minutes, then lower the setting to 180°C/ Fan 160°C/ Gas 4 and bake for another 30–40 minutes until the pastry is golden brown and the cherry filling is bubbling.

Leave the pie to cool to room temperature before serving, with scoops of vanilla ice cream.

Mississippi mud pie

THIS DECADENT, RICH PIE has a thick chocolate filling and a crumbly biscuit base, similar to a cheesecake. It is said to resemble the muddy banks of the Mississippi river – hence, its moniker – and remains a popular dessert in the southern states. There are many variations, but I prefer to make mine with good-quality chocolate rather than cocoa powder, which is commonly used by American home cooks.

SERVES 8

Biscuit base:
200g digestive biscuits
60g lightly salted butter, diced
60g good-quality dark chocolate, chopped

Chocolate filling:
180g good-quality dark chocolate, chopped
180g unsalted butter, diced
4 large eggs, lightly beaten
90g dark muscovado sugar
90g light muscovado sugar
200ml double cream

Topping:
100ml double cream, well chilled
2–3 tbsp icing sugar, to taste
chocolate shavings, to finish

To make the base, put the digestive biscuits into a resealable bag and lightly bash them with a rolling pin until evenly crushed. Tip into a large bowl. Melt the butter and chocolate together in a heatproof bowl set over a saucepan of gently simmering water. Stir until smooth, then take off the heat, pour onto the crushed biscuits and mix until evenly combined.

Tip the crumb mixture into a 23cm cake tin with removable base. Using the back of the spoon, press the mixture onto the base and up the sides of the tin to cover evenly. Chill to allow the base to firm up. Preheat the oven to 180°C/fan 160°C/Gas 4.

To make the filling, melt the chocolate and butter together in a bowl over simmering water (as above) and leave to cool slightly. In another large bowl, beat the eggs and muscovado sugars together, using an electric mixer, until thick and doubled in volume. Whisk in the cream, then fold through the melted chocolate and butter.

Pour the mixture over the biscuit base and bake in the oven for about 45 minutes until just firm. Allow to cool completely before removing from the tin. (If making in advance, remove from the fridge at least 30 minutes before serving as the chocolate filling will set and harden when cold.)

For the topping, whip the cream with icing sugar to taste until it holds soft peaks. Spread this over the top of the cooled pie and finish with a scattering of chocolate shavings. Cut into slices to serve.

Index